FORW...
AFTER
50 »

THE RISING REINVENTORS

REBECCA RONANE

Cover image by: Rhea Monte
Book design by: SWATT Books Ltd

Printed in the United Kingdom
First Printing, 2022

ISBN: 979-10-415-0500-5 (Paperback)
ISBN: 978-2-9585903-1-4 (eBook)

Rebecca Ronane
Maubec, 84660 France
rebeccaronane.com

DEDICATION

I dedicate this book to all the inspiring and supportive women
who've come into my life and made me who I am today.

* * *

To Una Coronna, who sent me on a life of adventures,
and Ruby McGuire, who has mentored me into being a
fearless, unstoppable female over fifty (and over sixty).

* * *

Last but not least, my partner, Alain Poirot, whose focus,
positivity and humour keep each day more exciting than the last.

DISCLAIMER

All efforts have been made to ensure that the content in this book is factual and accurate.

The book is designed to provide information and motivation to readers. It should not be used to diagnose or treat any health condition and as such is not intended to replace professional advice, medical or otherwise.

It is sold with the understanding that the author is not engaged to render any type of psychological, legal, or any other kind of professional advice. The content of the book is the sole expression of the author.

The author shall not be liable for any physical, psychological, emotional, financial or commercial damages, including but not limited to, special, incidental, consequential or other damages. The author's views and rights are the same: You are responsible for your own choices, actions, and results.

The author disclaims any liability arising directly or indirectly from the use of this book.

CONTENTS

FOREWORD

Rebecca has been a true inspiration to me around the subject of ageing. She is adamant that moving beyond fifty is the best time of your life, not something to fear.

We are what we tell ourselves. Rebecca helps you tell a powerful story about ageing, not one that limits you.

As women in the 50+ bracket, it's easy to fear getting older and what that will mean in terms of what you can achieve.

Rebecca teaches you that getting older isn't something to fear but something to celebrate. Passionate about how the media portrays ageing, she has been on a quest to help women appreciate their wisdom, often newfound freedom, and inner beauty.

Rebecca is on a mission to help women over fifty recognise that life really does begin after fifty. Fear around being judged disperses, and you get to create life on your terms.

She challenges us to view fifty-plus as the best years of our life and then shows us how to do it by sharing her life-coaching strategies and client success stories with us. The words come alive on the page when we hear from real-life women whose results have been dynamic and life changing.

In this her first book, Rebecca takes us on a journey of self-discovery. This book is a must-read for any of us going forward after fifty. She shares her wisdom and perspective on ageing and inspires you to reframe your mindset and be the *powerful* woman you can be.

Ruby McGuire, Business & Mindset Coach & Mentor
www.rubymcguire.com

MEET THE AUTHOR

My name is Rebecca Ronane, and I want to help you change how you think about ageing. I was born in Wimbledon in 1956. Today, I live under sunny skies in a small village in Provence, France, with my partner Alain and my dog Myrtle. I created a company called *Forward After Fifty*, a podcast show of the same name, and an international networking group, Network Provence.

My independence started at 17. After my parent's divorce, I departed the countryside of Surrey. First, I went to London to find a job. Then I started travelling while working as an au pair. Gifted with an unexpected opportunity to earn, learn and travel at 28, I began my career in the travel industry, where I took groups of tourists to many countries worldwide.

I then left city life to live in the South of France, I was 39, and unlike many, I wasn't looking to live my dream life in Provence; it just happened.

A challenge came with a breast cancer diagnosis in my early fifties, then losing a job I imagined would last forever. It was then I started to buy into the ageing story.

What I didn't know then was that doors seemingly closing were unseen opportunities.

My curiosity, open-mindedness and an advert for a coaching course opened the door to a different chapter in my journey. Since training as a coach, I have set up my businesses, *Forward After Fifty* and Network Provence. As a result, I have two websites, two podcast shows and not one but several businesses to my name. This means that I have experienced that moving forward after fifty has the potential to be the most exciting part of your life.

A suggestion in 2021 that I write a book was a little like looking down on someone else's life and ambitions, as it had never been on my agenda. My life story has come with surprises, opportunities and challenges. Of course, it helps to be a little impulsive and desire to be challenged.

Now, all of this didn't just happen. It's taken years to create plans, do the inner work to master shifts in my mindset, and time to do the actual work. Nevertheless, I love ageing, and I want you to do so too. Like everyone, I've had trials and tribulations, but I choose to focus on the positives of the ageing process.

You have more superpowered years ahead of you than you imagine. But unfortunately, we're not living in a world prepared for so many healthy, innovative and passionate women over fifty, and it's up to us to fix that!

This book will give you insights into ways you might be limiting yourself in how you think and talk about ageing. Change your mindset around ageing today – start associating ageing with generating instead of degenerating, and then the magic begins.

I know that anything is possible for women who want to move *Forward After Fifty*. So, I've written this book to share reflections and thoughts about ageing.

I want to move you away from the negative ageing bias to recognise the incredible opportunities a woman like you can have.

Women over fifty are a force to be reckoned with. My mission is to convince you and the rest of the world of this fact so that opportunities are plentiful for you as you reinvent your life and step into your superpowers.

Here's to your reinvention.

Rebecca

WHY READ THIS BOOK?

I lost my job in my mid-fifties after dedicating over twenty years to a business that wasn't my own. Yet, my commitment had created customer confidence, leading to repeat business – a familiar story in the world of work.

Suddenly I felt older. Why? Because my friends suggested that it wasn't easy to get work 'at my age'. This limited thinking triggered lots of negativity. I didn't want to change careers, but feeling lost, I began to worry about finances, pushing me to apply for work.

I was pleasantly surprised that it came my way; however, it didn't feel right, and alarm bells rang when I thought of my future. I knew that if age was limiting, I needed to make the most of my time. So, I now take control and plan my future.

With a reinvention plan in place, I studied and invested in myself, getting needed support. I chose to listen to my heart and intuition, instead of listening to others. As a result, I smashed through my comfort zone, built confidence around managing my finances, and started to celebrate my age instead of using it as an excuse. I went on to set up a business, maximising my newfound skillset, and I am now helping other women feel confident around their future selves.

As part of the research for this book, I spoke to ten women about their experiences with ageing. I'll be sharing their thoughts throughout the book.

This book is dedicated to all women who need to reclaim their superpowers, stop people-pleasing and embrace ageing after fifty and beyond.

As my friend would say, "It's far too easy to fall into the stereotypical traps and misconceptions about ageing, women's abilities, and what is beautiful".

My wish for you is what one of my interviewees shared as part of a conversation:

"The difference between who I am now and who I was when I was younger is that I was very much being the type of person I needed to be to create the life I wanted. Whereas now, I'm not prepared to compromise on that. I want the life I want. I don't want to have to pretend to be anybody else to get it!"

Carol

RISING REINVENTORS

Throughout the book, you will find 'Rising Reinventors' graphics. I believe we, as women, can be a powerful force for good. I like to collectively call us Rising Reinventors. We can reinvent the way people perceive ageing.

I see Rising Reinventors as part of the up-and-coming movement of women over fifty who feel they have the same rights as every age group to rise up and be heard.

We've got a great deal to say and to contribute and want to have access to all the opportunities out in the world – a reference to frustrated wise elders looking for respect rather than ending up on the retirement heap.

A rising reinvention is a new way of looking at age and oneself with pride and excitement. Generate and regenerate, not degenerate.

Rising relates to the phoenix and is a reference to what is happening in today's world, albeit slowly yet happily surely.

I hope these graphics will stop you in your tracks and get you thinking about how you can play your part (large or small) in reinventing the way people think about ageing.

Part One

REBECCA RONANE

INTRODUCTION

In Part 1, we are going to explore ageist views and how your values and beliefs can shape your life.

In Chapter 1, *Let's Get Rid of Ageism*, you will discover what's happening worldwide on the topic of ageing.

In Chapter 2, *The Phoenix Effect*, you will learn how an ancient myth can help you on your reinvention journey over fifty.

In Chapter 3, *Values – Your Superpower*, you will start to uncover what makes you tick and how you can use this knowledge to empower and enrich your life.

In Chapter 4, *Mindset – Your Secret Weapon*, you will learn how to use your mindset wisely to inform your decisions and future self.

In Chapter 5, *Wellbeing in Your Hands*, you will discover ways to improve your health and wellbeing so that an ageing body doesn't define you.

Chapter 1

LET'S GET RID OF AGEISM

What age are you?

In this chapter, we're redefining what 'old' actually is. You'll start to recognise and eliminate any ageist views you may have acquired or have had imposed upon you. We still live in a world and a culture which is, as you will see, infected with ageism, making it incredibly difficult not to take on some level of ageist bias. Rooting this out is the start-point to kick-start your reinvention.

If you're not ageist in any way, then that's wonderful. You can inspire others to be the same. However, it's all too easy to not even be aware that you are being ageist. In which case, some of what I have to say might feel uncomfortable. My intention is not to be judgmental but to raise awareness of how you might be playing your part in ageism and to help you recognise what you can do differently.

If we didn't have birthdays, we wouldn't know what age we were. So, for example, at the time of writing, I'm 65, but I certainly don't think of myself as old. To me, 'old' is when you start to slow down and lose mobility.

We can fall into the trap of observing this slowing down period with dread. We can even get to the point that we start to expect a decline, despite knowing that not everyone ages in the same way. We can often find it hard to identify with our actual age as we are still young in our heads. Indeed, the interviewees I spoke to would say they felt a good 10-20 years younger than their actual age. Ask yourself: what age do you feel you are? You might be surprised with your answer.

Almost everything in this book will help you feel better about ageing if you **actively** do something about it. Firstly, stop speaking about age negatively.

"If you don't age, you can't gain experience and wisdom."

Colette

Be more like the Blue Zone super-agers. Scientific studies have pinpointed several areas in the world where the average lifespan is well above the norm. These are known as Blue Zones, a term identified by Gianni Pes, Michel Poulain and Dan Buettner. Five zones have been identified, namely Okinawa (Japan); Sardinia (Italy); Nicoya (Costa Rica); Icaria (Greece); and Loma Linda (California, U.S.)

Interestingly, these Blue Zones are often situated within agricultural communities or in places where the topography requires more walking and steps to climb. What's interesting is that all super-agers have similarities – they have moderate diets, partake in plenty of physical activity, and have a thriving community spirit.

The Blue Zone longevity recipe

- Stay social
- Exercise your mind and body
- Eat with care

And the great news? All these ingredients are free and doable.

Remaining independent

Concern with ageing is taking a different direction; those in authority no longer concentrate on homes for the aged; they are turning to how they can keep you at work.

"The traditional story about ageing is that as we age, we slow down, become trapped in our habits, and forget to play. The good news is that we can avoid this, and we can all learn to use our brains to change our age. Who doesn't want to live longer?"

Jim Kwik

Concern regarding independence is an issue mentioned frequently by my interviewees. Superpowered women want independence. We expect age to take our independence away, whether physically, mentally, or financially. Often a cultural attitude means that we believe losing our independence is inevitable; however, times have changed.

You have choices: you can sit back and wait for age to get you, or you can do something about it.

Ageist prejudices

Ageism can affect everyone, both young and old. Different age groups can feel treated unjustly and not heard. They can be stereotyped into a categorisation of less importance.

I jumped for joy when I learned that menopause is, at last, being given some serious attention by the UK government. Yet, age categorisation and terms such as 'middle-aged' are still bandied around by the media.

How does your age make you feel different?

A poll by the University of Michigan on ageism returned statistics that two in three older adults reported exposure to ageist messages in their day-to-day lives. This included often hearing, seeing, and reading jokes about old age, suggesting that older adults and ageing are unattractive or undesirable. Furthermore, it says that ageism can directly affect our physical and mental wellbeing.

The likelihood that younger people view you as someone who needs help with your mobile phone or anything remotely technical is high. For example, I recently attended an online conference where the speaker told us to ask a teenager if we didn't understand the technology. If you let someone else do it, then that's one fat chance that you will never learn to do it for yourself.

Spending money and time on looking younger is encouraged from an early age, but it has been proven that most over sixty-year-olds, despite ageism battles, feel more at ease with themselves and therefore happier. This happy state debunks the myth of lost youth, whatever that means. For me, being younger was a time of feeling lost, not knowing what to do and at a loss as to how to deal with spots and greasy hair. I'd rather be in the position of knowing who I am now.

The value of intergeneration

Intergeneration is where something exists or affects several generations. In this instance, it's about people of all ages connecting.

So how can intergeneration affect your life after fifty?

A new career will mean more interaction with people of all ages. We are in a time when most people over fifty will be healthier and still working, and many generations are mixing and working together.

RISING REINVENTORS

Letting go of biases and embracing a changing world is part and parcel of moving into your superpower time, although this might initially seem uncomfortable and challenging. For me, this has turned out to be the most exciting period of life, and it could be for you too. Of course, exploring this unknown territory is not for everyone, but if you think you have at fifty a chance of thirty more productive years plus, then you want to make the most of them.

Modernising your thinking, knowledge and curiosity is progress. Make the most of these crucial years of your life. The wisdom of elders with the freshness of youth is the perfect combination.

The other side of the coin is 'non-intergeneration' which "contributes to prejudice, social, cultural and economic discrepancies", according to dictionary.com.

Crossing the generation divide leads to mutual respect and an evolvement of new dynamic ideas.

Intergenerational businesses

Could you create a business that will aid intergeneration?

How about creating a business with your child/children? The family business has been around for a long time and is one with a proven track record of stability and success. When I think of a family business, I think of a long-established business, but why not try something new? The different skillsets that you can both bring to the table are endless.

If the idea of working with your child/children fills your heart with dread, what about working with other people who are a different age to you?

In my research for this book, I came across Cirkel, a US innovation focused on business networking but targeted explicitly to allow all ages to exchange business ideas. On their website (at the time of writing, at cirkel.co) their introductory proposition states: "Join a community of professionals aged 20-70+ and access wisdom from other generations". That sounds a great idea to me.

I had a conversation with one of their community managers who said: "We believe in the power of intergenerational work. We have seen the value, magic and beauty behind connecting generations especially in a world where ageism exists across the board. It is something that we are actively looking at to change the narrative".

Intergenerational living

Intergenerational living is seen by many as a solution to fit all ages. Living with people younger than you can help to fill the gap of loneliness by bringing people together. They can add fresh energy into your life, and you can bring wisdom to theirs. Condos (community housing spaces) have their place when designed with older age in mind; however, I believe a housing development with several generations living together can be much more beneficial for everyone. This could be a valuable part of the solution to ageism.

Individual homes/apartments with shared spaces and facilities are slowly emerging. In all but western countries, extended families tend to be the norm. Rather than living surrounded by the same age group as in retirement living complexes, intergenerational living becomes more like a variant on the extended family where different age groups can come together and share ideas. We are starting to tap into this wisdom of the past again.

As a shining example of this, I came across Lasell Village (lasellvillage.com), a senior living community, situated on the campus of Lasell University in Massachusetts. The concept is seniors living in one- or two-bedroom homes, which comes with rules in the shape of a commitment to taking 450 hours of learning and fitness each year. This isn't something new – it's been active for twenty years. The students' ages span from young adults to people over 100 years old, an excellent example of intergenerational living.

The Netherlands has always had issues with accommodation, particularly for students. An innovative project started in 2012 by Humanitas (humanitasdeventer.nl/) has seen several students living in care homes for seniors. The students converse, connect, walk with, prepare meals and eat with the care home residents, and live in the house in return for free rent. In the next 10 years, I'm optimistic that we will see more intergeneration, whether it's in business or living circumstances.

Avoiding categorisation and stereotyping

Let's work towards connection rather than categorisation.

"Working to make the world more age-friendly is an essential and urgent part of our changing demographics." So says The World Health Organisation (WHO – who.int/), as, by 2050, there will be over 2 billion people over sixty on our planet.

Our parents' age meant retirement at sixty-plus. This has now changed. The worthiness of people over fifty is not being tapped into, even though the future depends on it.

This needs to change.

We need to create age-friendly environments. That means consideration of intergenerational opportunity, valuing people in work no matter what age, whether applying for a job, creating or running a business. Living needs need to be recognised.

Mindset also needs addressing and part of the problem is seeing our self-worth. Self-worth can be a challenge; being surrounded by ageing negativity means you either toughen up or do some inner work on yourself. In my case, I invested in personal development, which has led to my positive ageing outlook.

We need to change our ageist views – so many of us are ageist.

The United Nations (un.org/) has identified ageism as an issue that will harm the economy if we don't recognise its harmful effects. Young and old must have mutual respect. If qualified, everyone needs to have an equal opportunity to apply for a job and know that their experience is a worthwhile addition.

People have told my generation that ageing comes with a decline in cognitive thinking. The word cognitive, as explained online, means 'the mental action or process of acquiring knowledge and understanding through thought, experience, and the senses'. It is, in essence, the ability to perceive and react, process and understand, store and retrieve information, make decisions and produce appropriate responses.

Therefore, our experience is a tool worth its weight in gold. But unfortunately, due to our cultural upbringing and the media portraying us as a nuisance to society, many of us expect the worst. Therefore, physically and mentally manifesting a scenario of decline is a dangerous occupation.

"When I first started this job, I cried in the loo. I was thrown in to the deep end thinking I was older than everyone else."

Kath

Cultural differences

As I started researching this book, it struck me the various cultural differences on the process of ageing and how it relates to work.

In Japan, there is a deep respect for others and age is revered. People of every age are encouraged to work. There are employment agencies for the over-sixties that train and promote more senior workers. This creates happiness, fulfilment, and extra income. Working is considered a contribution to better health and to society in general.

Finland is another country with a rapidly ageing demographic, but with an age-embracing approach. The government is investing in keeping their ageing population healthy, with courses available for all on good diet, exercise classes, and physical and mental wellbeing.

Italy has a fast-ageing population. Its social services struggle for many reasons. Historically, Italians of all ages have emigrated to find opportunities elsewhere and are not being replaced. Women often don't have children due to a lack of money or support from social services. Eighty per cent of the country's carers are not Italian, and many of them would rather be elsewhere. Italian policy has kept away foreign workers. Currently, the future of ageing across many western countries is rather bleak, particularly where there is a lack of investment.

One possible way to remedy the situation in the short term would be to redefine what 'old' is. In Finland, a debate is ongoing as to whether being 65 is 'old' in this day and age. Some experts argue that old age now starts at 80, with people in their sixties falling into the 'silver economy'. People who can still contribute to the workplace and be active are increasingly working into their later years.

Ageism is all around us

After reading a post by the United Nations that people over fifty are held back by ageism from creating businesses, making career changes, going for jobs and contributing to the economy, I saw this headline: *One in Two of Us Are Ageist.*

The article discusses the ever-increasing ageing population, creating burdens and costs. On the one hand, doomsayers are telling the world we drain societies. On the other hand, the word is we are an 'untapped cash cow'. These so-called financial drainers will become the financial boomers.

RISING REINVENTORS

The portrayal of what people over fifty can't do is more popular in the media than what they can do. After all, we know that gloom sells. My personal experience has been that both my parents sailed into their eighties with creative capabilities. My father tried his hand at writing and my mother continued her drawing. What they didn't have were marketing skills or the knowledge to sell their work.

If updating skills and or intergenerational businesses were encouraged, people way into their eighties could be adding to the economy and to their own lives. In my mother's ninetieth year, she created a calendar with paintings and ideas from the region we live in. We sold some to friends, and I know it could have become a successful product with some marketing, preparation and know-how. My mother's remark, "If only I'd done this earlier", has a clear message indeed.

Stop writing yourself and older people off. Embrace your age instead.

The following lines from an article in AARP International (aarpinternational.org) on how governments must make changes sum up this adaptation to how humanity is evolving:

"People are leading longer, more productive lives; they can make a more significant lifetime economic contribution than members of past generations ever could."

The article talks about flexible working and retirement policies that work. The way we work is changing rapidly. I started writing this book in 2021 when, as a result of the global pandemic, hybrid working has become standard for so many of us, working partly at home and partly in an office. We no longer need to spend hours travelling to and from work, which is excellent news. This is proving to be a permanent shift in the attitude towards working practices and could be one of the most empowering changes in recent years in allowing older people to extend their working life.

Anyone over fifty may well feel disconnected from investing in themselves, if you take a look across the media and the high street. You could believe that the only valid purchaser on the planet is under thirty-five. Have you ever had a buying experience where a clothing assistant presumed you were buying for someone else, such as your daughter, rather than yourself? How dare you be in a clothes shop where the designs are aimed at below thirty! Have you been herded towards the anti-wrinkle cream in the cosmetics department?

It's not a surprise that the under-thirties dominate the advertising world. Yet, these worlds would be smashing their sales targets if intergeneration were the future answer to marketing. Imagine an attitude of inclusivity, with an all-age, gender, and race perspective in the media. Until then, youth sells.

Ageism and exercise

Exercise equals living longer and in good health. The popularity of fitness clubs is increasing as more people understand they do have a choice to live a healthier life if they exercise. However, even before you put a foot past the door, some clubs can make you feel that you must be or look like an Olympian to be accepted.

Marketing portraying youthful men and women with rippling muscles can be off-putting at any age, even more so if you are a beginner.

We need more people such as *Train with Joan*, whose story shows how, at seventy, you can reverse so much of the bad health in your life. Joan MacDonald took her health into her own hands through exercise and nutrition. Although her daughter is a coach with a gym, Joan could be you or me.

Joan was an overweight, highly medicated and out-of-breath seventy-year-old whose daughter begged her to try to take her future to a better place. Please take a look at the trainwithjoanofficial.com website to see the transformation Joan has brought about in herself, and now inspires millions of older women to do the same. Imagine if advertisers used someone like 'before and after' Joan as the face of the fitness world. It would not only boost the income of the fitness industry, adding a whole extra sector of membership and engagement, but also improve longevity, which could decrease the old fear for the future of a planet heavily populated by the over-fifties who are often viewed as a drain on resources.

The fitness chain, David Lloyd, is proactively employing fitness trainers over fifty, so that each club has at least one fitness trainer aged over fifty to attract the over-fifties into their clubs. A gym ought to be a place with the opportunity to have a personal trainer to hold your hand to health. Walking into a club where all ages are represented is good for morale and making connections.

Make women over fifty visible!

However, age is not limited to the fitness industry. The cosmetics industry has traditionally been the Queen of Anti-Ageing. Few companies have dared to market a face over thirty, let alone over fifty.

The cosmetic industry comes out tops for its ability to discredit ageing. The industry has instilled fear by targeting women to repel age at all costs, so the effect can be devastating physically and mentally when the wrinkles do arrive. Here, the myth of fabulous youth is promoted to make us feel devalued and loosen our purse strings. Say NO to this nonsense and YES to the superpower of wrinkles!

"Wrinkles should merely indicate where the smiles have been."
Mark Twain

My wish is for marketing to target us to value and celebrate ourselves, which will encourage us to continue purchasing. Next comes another area where youth sells.

In the world of fashion, once you are over fifty you will struggle to find yourself represented. Does a slim, tall 16 to 21-year-old influence your fashion choices when you're over fifty? Once over fifty, you will have probably found your style and your identity, and this should be represented out there!

Most of my shopping is online; I shop at Uniqlo, a casual wear company. I don't see any pictures of over-fifties women when searching for clothes. Are we not supposed to be interested in clothes anymore? Would Uniqlo be horrified that my 91-year-old mother is wearing their casual clothes?

Other well-known brands such as Zara and H&M have a smattering of older models, but you may miss them unless you look closely. Ironically, many of the world's iconic fashion designers are women who are over fifty.

Why aren't Miuccia Prada and Diane von Furstenberg, both in their seventies, and many more, rocking the fashion world with fashion shows for over-fifties? After all, the audience with the money to buy these clothes is predominantly an older age group.

Using age as an excuse

Please don't use age as an excuse! It feeds into ageist views. The problem is that if you constantly talk negatively about ageing, you can also start to believe it and make even more excuses to put your life on hold.

So often I hear the age excuse used both on and offline. When I hear it, my teeth start to grind, and I think, please don't include me in your age excuses. Yes, it's common in our culture, yet it has no place anymore.

 **RISING REINVENTORS**

I hear people talking disparagingly about ageing all the time. Maybe you recognise yourself in the following statements:

"I'm too old to:
- Do sport
- Lose weight
- Learn technology

- Learn new skills
- Take a risk
- Change
- Make that dream come true."

And the list goes on.

Listen to how you and others speak about ageing. Choose to spend time in good company with people that talk about ageing positively.

"I can still do whatever I want to do. I don't feel I've got any barriers that stop me."

Maxine

Instead of buying into ageist beliefs, I'd like to encourage you to adopt what I call the Phoenix Effect, which we will explore next. Before we do, I have a question for you.

Now that we have explored a number of areas relating to ageism: *How ageist are you?*

Age is irrelevant. It's how you live as you age which defines how you move *Forward After Fifty*.

CHAPTER REFLECTION

So now you know the recipe to a long healthy life as lived in the Blue Zone: eat moderately, connect and exercise.

You may also now be more conscious of your ageist habits, in yourself and others, and how these don't serve your reinvention.

TAKE ACTION

Start to notice if you have ageist habits. If you do, choose something you would like to change.

What one step can you take to improve your habits in this area? i.e., *I will stop joining in negative conversations with my friends around ageing. Instead, I will inspire them to think differently along with me.*

Remember, behaviour doesn't change overnight. However, one small change can have a ripple effect.

In the next chapter, we will explore reinvention and why NOW is a perfect age for you to embrace the 'Phoenix Effect'.

Chapter 2

THE PHOENIX EFFECT

The phoenix is an immortal bird spoken of in Greek mythology, and over the centuries in many other cultures. Having a close association with the sun, the bird was said to end one life in flames and begin the next by rising from the ashes, a symbol of eternal renewal. For me this is a beautiful evocation of how we can reinvent ourselves as we approach ageing.

I believe that everyone can choose to reinvent themselves at any point in life. I like to call this reinvention the Phoenix Effect. This is why the phoenix is part of my branding.

RISING REINVENTORS

While reinvention can be exciting, it's not always without challenge. In this chapter, I will discuss how to deal with these challenges head-on. But, first, you'll discover how to keep your negative bias at bay and limiting beliefs under control, so that you are unstoppable.

When you become a Rising Reinventor,
you feel confident in sharing your
wisdom, not worrying what others think.

Creating new roles

Understanding what makes you tick can be invaluable as you reinvent yourself. In Chapter 3, we will be exploring values, a great tool to help you understand yourself better.

I'll be honest with you – reinvention wasn't a word in my dictionary when I turned fifty. I was in a reasonably good place, and the bits that weren't ideal I could put up with for an easy life. Now, those fifteen years since I settled for that so-called easy life have become some of the most life-changing.

That easy life of mine became disrupted by a sequence of rapid-fire disappointments. A routine mammogram turned into a breast cancer diagnosis, followed by losing what I had come to believe was a 'job for life'. I was fifty-five and unprepared to start all over again. My confidence crashed. I began to go with the flow of ageist negativity, of "You're over-fifty and finished". It was at this point I recognised the opportunity for change.

Unfortunately, I didn't know anything about core values at that time. These are the guiding gems you need to pull you out of a mess. However, one of my top five values, that of learning, began to rise to the surface. A fairy godmother appeared, namely my good friend Colette, who invited me to join her English teaching workshop. As a result, I started a Teaching English as a Foreign Language (TEFL) course. Although I've never used this certificate, it put me on the track of believing that I could obtain new skills.

Simultaneously, Colette and I talked about creating a business together. While discussing a name for our company, the word 'coach' appeared. This word led me to the world of self-discovery, becoming a life coach and running a networking group. At fifty-five, none of these things had been on my agenda. Instead, I was now embarking on a journey of creating new roles for myself.

"My children have left home, what's my new role?"

Janine

Have big dreams

Daring to dream big may feel far-fetched and beyond becoming a reality, yet sticking to a vision of your big juicy goals can create your future self. And yes, you do have a great future ahead of you if you choose to believe.

As an infant, you are allowed to live in a world of make-believe, and then at a certain point, an adult will tell you to stop daydreaming and start concentrating. There's a lot out there about the dos and don'ts of daydreaming. Do you see yourself doing something different, yet making a start seems overwhelming?

In a discussion with a group of friends, a couple of us mentioned we were writing books. One piped up, "But who will read it?" I replied that I would never write it if that thought had entered my mind. Who would do anything if they mulled over how it would be received?

I've been disappointed on occasions when something didn't go according to plan, but it hasn't put me off following my dreams. Why do I feel like that? Principally my goal is for me. If I don't achieve it, I will have let myself down, leading to regrets.

"The biggest challenge, I think, is to still believe that you can still change your life. Whatever your life is, you can still go out and do it."

Carol

Secondly, my goal is driven by being of benefit to others. You may be thinking that sounds selfish, asking who does she think she is? What makes you think your dreams will benefit me or others? These were the thoughts I carried for many years, including unworthiness, telling myself that if it's not perfect, I'll look a fool. I believed that if what I created was not world-changing, then nobody would listen.

This brings to mind a friend who has been writing books for many years, yet she kept all her material to herself to calm her fear of rejection. That fear of rejection, sense of a need for perfection, agonising self-doubt and ultimately all that regret, all of it is unnecessary.

We're all different. We each have a huge amount of experience and wisdom. Allow yourself to dream in a grand style to create your reinvention – don't hold back!

RISING REINVENTORS

Karen had always considered herself creative but had only done art at school. So, she began to reinvent herself and spent time learning more about painting. As a result, she now has her own YouTube channel and following on Instagram and Facebook. She teaches art classes locally, and during the pandemic lockdown, she taught classes online. Karen says she wants to make something of the rest of her life and not live with regrets. She is a great example of how you can develop your skills and learn something new.

"It's okay to live my dream, no matter what other people think. We can begin to step up and create our own journey."

Janine

Create a plan

The next exciting step is creating a plan. This stage can be challenging and fun.

In my journey, I work 1:1 with a business coach and mastermind group to keep me accountable, help me to strategise, and encourage me to achieve my goals. If you're not familiar with coaching, a coach essentially asks you questions to help you recognise unhelpful thinking patterns and create change through setting goals and taking action.

When I entered the world of studying to be a coach, I'd never had a coach myself, and on reflection, I hadn't invested in my self-development.

It wasn't long after setting up my own business that my need to know more and improve on what I wanted to share with others came to the forefront.

I've never looked back, only forward. There's that moment when, after spending time gaining your wisdom, you arrive at a point of putting it into some form. I've learnt more about myself in the last ten years than at any other time. Personal development has given me the strength to take risks I'd never have made without someone, in this case, my coach, objectively cheering me on.

Before I talk about a reinvention plan, let's learn what a couple of ladies have to say when I asked them the following questions:

If you could be/do anything, what would it be?

"Oh, I would be a speaker on stage at corporate events, retreats and schools. I would like to inspire women and young people. However, I do really do that in a small way with my podcast show. I would love to be able to share the different phases and stages in life and how it impacts us as we gain experience. I'd also like to share where we keep ourselves playing small, instead of living life in full."

Janine

What have you been saying you want to do, but haven't yet done?

"Learn a language. I've often thought that learning Spanish would be great, and I've never got around to it for some reason. I've just put it on hold."

Maxine

Your reinvention plan

If you need a reinvention plan, here are a few steps to get you started:

1. Write down your overall goal, i.e., *Become a Yoga instructor.*
2. Break this into small subtasks, i.e., *Research Yoga courses, choose level of training, create space in diary for Yoga practice.*

3. Write down any actions you can take to achieve your goal. To avoid overwhelm, keep your tasks small and achievable – this is key to your success, i.e., *Spend one hour researching courses, speak to an instructor about their journey, block out 2 hours in your diary.*

4. Most people work to the annual calendar. However, breaking your year into quarters or months can help you stay focused and make everything feel more attainable. You can then break down your week into time blocks if that works for you.

Be sure to set time aside for your self-care. My coach introduced me to the Pomodoro Technique, where you work in twenty-five-minute blocks of time. In this time, you are focused on one task. This system helps if you are like me, someone who is easily distracted. It keeps out the noise of chores or social media or anything else that is on your to-do list.

I use a whiteboard to write my daily tasks; I then number each one in order. Crossing your tasks off at the end of the day gives you a sense of achievement and a reason to reward yourself.

You may already be a planner and find it easy to stay focused, and you perhaps don't have too many distractions or life chores that get in the way, or you might be, like me, somewhat impulsive. Of course, this impulsiveness has its benefits sometimes, but it needs to be reined in and disciplined by creating a plan.

Any day is a good day to start something you've been putting off.

Recognise your planning style

Different people plan in different ways. You might recognise yourself in one of the following two characterisations, the Planner or the Non-Planner:

Planners

- love planning
- like milestones
- do not like plans changing
- hate disruptions
- focus on one thing before moving on
- are considered decision-makers
- like precise timekeeping
- work in time blocks
- are constantly trying to improve time
- stick to their commitments.

Non-Planners

- are spontaneous – why plan? Plans change
- love change
- love disruption – it gives energy and mixes up projects
- are quick decision-makers
- like flowing time-streams
- are not keen on structure if not getting results
- like trying new things
- can be challenging for people to pin you down.

These descriptions are only a bit of fun, used with permission from an online programme from my coach. However, you will likely identify with one type over the other. It's worth considering what factors you can take from either kind that might help you create a plan.

If your plan includes work you are not familiar with or even interested in, delegate this to experts. This doesn't have to cost the earth and allows you to focus on your core skills and interests.

Remember, sometimes life isn't about the pre-planned. Unnecessary misadventures can also be marvellous!

CHAPTER REFLECTION

If you take anything away from this chapter, I would love it to be the following 3 key points:

1. Dream on a large scale
2. Create a plan of action
3. Choose to challenge your thinking about moving *Forward After Fifty*.

Recognising that everyone is unique can feel uncomfortable, and you may wonder what makes you different. Yet you are unique, whether you recognise that yet or not.

TAKE ACTION

Are you ready to make the conscious choice to become a Rising Reinventor, part of a 'movement' where the negativity of ageing becomes a thing of the past?

If you are, then create your Phoenix Effect action plan.

In the next chapter I will reveal a priceless tool to help you understand yourself.

"Expect the unexpected, and whenever possible, be the unexpected."

Lynda Barry

Chapter 3

VALUES – YOUR SUPERPOWERS

The essence of you is your core values. If you are asking what your values are, then you're not alone. I had no idea what values were until I started my life-coaching journey. Knowing them now has been a game-changer for me. This chapter will explain values, their importance, and why you need to know yours to activate your superpowers.

Values help you to understand:

- What makes you tick and why
- What you do, and why you do it
- Who you want to be with and who you don't want to be with.

These are the essential keys to living a life that works.

Your values are in themselves what I like to call a superpower.

I learned about my values through an exercise with my coach where you explore what's most important to you in life – these are then what you define as your values.

Defining core values

My top five values are *learning, energy, challenge, connection,* and *nature.* Learning my values was a revelation to me. They have enabled me to make sense of myself. Let me give some examples of my values in action:

My curiosity as I delve into something unknown feeds into my love of *learning.*

A surge of powerful *energy* at a networking meeting combines with the joy of making *connections.*

When I experience a sense of boredom, I know that I lack *challenge.*

My spirit rising as I walk through the forest is brought on by *nature.*

When I come out of my Pilates reform class, I'm on a high due to the *challenge,* group *energy,* the *connection* with others, *learning* a new exercise and or something about myself.

Take a moment to imagine my fellow gym classmate who has experienced the same class yet comes out complaining bitterly. Their lack of enthusiasm could be because they are only there as they view exercise as vital for their health. None of my values may apply to them. Instead, they might prefer to be at home reading a book.

I could become judgmental and ask myself why this moaning individual comes along. But, instead, I focus on my needs. I choose to concentrate on how the class fits in with my essence (my core values). It is not about others.

We spend a lot of time understanding other people who come into our lives, whether friends or family. Yet, we could divert that energy into trying to understand the most important person, you.

You could probably avoid many situations that don't make you feel happy or fulfilled; imagine how amazing that would be! By understanding yourself, you can prevent rubbish relationships, time spent arguing, wasted energy and crappy jobs.

"I am finding inner peace and doing what I want to do. Being organised and seeing people that I want to see and know."

Kath

Being aware of your core values empowers you to make choices that feel right, whether professional or emotional. They help you to become aligned with all aspects of your life and discover who you truly are.

"There's always somebody somewhere doing what you're doing. But in fact, they're not doing it the way you're doing it. We all have to something unique to offer."

Lisa

Understand yourself

What difference can it make understanding your values?

A huge difference. Firstly, there is a realisation of who you are, why you do what you do, why you like some people and why you don't like others. You begin to uncover what makes you happy, sad, excited, emotional, cross, inspired, and so much more.

"The deep connection I have with who I am is honest now. The critical difference between who I am now and who I was then is that I'm not prepared to compromise on the life I want. I don't want to pretend to be anybody to get it."

Carol

Below is a 'word cloud' showing a list of some core values. You can find many lists online if you want to explore this further. Choose five words from the image below, and then notice how the core value words you've chosen make you feel.

You may think, hmm, challenge is the last thing in the world that would make me feel good. But, on the other hand, the core value of security may light you up, which could mean a comfortable house, having enough money and not too much change in your family circumstances.

Find your unique top five values and start to be conscious of where they stand in your life.

Identifying your core values

There are many processes to help you identify your key values. Here's a simple exercise, as an example, to find the values which are important to you:

- Make a list of 15-20 things you need in life to feel complete, i.e., *adventure, family, learning.*
- Next, prioritise your list and rate the items according to how important they are to you.
- Then prioritise again to get your top 10 most important things.
- Finally, drill down to your top five. It can be surprising that your top five are not always what you expect.

Once you're aware of those top five values, you have empowered yourself to live authentically. Decision-making becomes more straightforward and logical. Even if you believe you have made the wrong decision, you'll understand that it was for reasons that made sense, as it will have aligned with your values.

Your values are like a guiding system you've longed to have. Over time, you will wish you had tapped into these self-awareness tools years ago. If only we were taught this valuable life tool in school.

"I feel good about getting older because I have no regrets; I've lived my best life. I've done some incredible things over the years. So, I can look back now at my life and feel good about it. And when I reflect on all my core values, I feel I've lived by them, which is important to me."

Maxine

As Janice has said to me, as you get older, you try to enjoy the spirit of your life more. She enjoys writing and her "crazy way of photography". Janice feels that bringing out her artistic side has helped her be authentic. She says sometimes she prefers just being on her own, without the pressure of always getting made up or being 'on stage'.

Values help decision-making

You make your best decisions when they are in alignment with your values.

Knowing your core values guides you to make the best decisions to live. This understanding also helps you understand past choices. You will understand why some decisions have been difficult to make and why you have regretted some past decisions that didn't feel right.

Your guiding core values will reveal the why and help you make better decisions in the future. For example, they can guide you in making more significant life decisions, such as finding the right job, a partnership, or any situation of any kind. Once you know your top five values, the easier making decisions will be.

Values in conflict

An argument at work, with family, friends, or your partner. Don't you sometimes wish everyone had the same opinion as you?! What makes you angry will be completely different to what makes other people angry.

Why do people argue? According to various articles, the answers are many, ranging from a lack of wanting to compromise, a lack of empathy and power struggles, to lack of respect, irritation, and or even just a lack of sleep. Some people like to pick a fight.

Everything will make sense if you know your core values and the person or people you are in conflict with. What a pity that pre-nuptial vows don't include the exercise of finding out your top values! Perhaps there would be lower divorce rates! Respect for other people's feelings could prevent conflict or help you to understand why you are at odds with somebody else.

When conflict arises, stop and think. Everyone is different. If the other person is authentic, and therefore able to say what they truly think, they may disagree with you. A difference of opinion can be illuminating and should in fact be welcomed in an open-minded way. However, if you understand each other's values, 'where you are coming from', there's a better chance of a more rounded and considered discussion, leading to a harmonious relationship, even if your values are different. It's all about having respect for the views of others, once you know their values.

So, if you are going to live by your core values, then you need to argue your point because what is at stake is part of who you are. However, if you hit a brick wall, take a step back and make sure you take into account the other person's perspective. Ask yourself what values might be coming into play in their life.

Imagine a partnership where one side (Person A) has the five core values of responsibility, family, security, creativity and kindness, and the other person (Person B) has adventure, entertainment, success, diversity and creativity as theirs.

If this couple had a dispute about money, with Person A saying that Person B needs to get a stable job, it is easy to understand how that would arise, given their widely differing values. However, understanding your own values and those of people close to you is at least a good start-point to understanding why an argument has arisen and how it might be resolved.

Conflict at work might arise when your values include kindness, honesty, generosity, nature and integrity. Imagine being in a situation where your company/boss's branding is supposedly about being ethical and ecological, including donating money to nature projects. This may even be why you chose to work there. Yet, you find out that the boss flies from place to place in a private jet and sacks people you believe are acting with integrity and serving the company well. If the actions and direction of the company you work for are so out of line with your values, there comes a point where to carry on working there is being hypocritical to yourself and your values. Only by being clear on your values can you make correct decisions in your life.

The benefits of understanding yourself are endless.

Avoid people who will not serve your purpose in life. Find an ideal environment where starting a business or project creates happiness and satisfaction.

CHAPTER REFLECTION

You now understand more about what makes you tick, why values are important and how you can use them to enhance your superpowers.

TAKE ACTION

Spend some time discovering what your core values are. Then, using the word cloud image, think about which values you need to have in your life to be you, and prioritise them. Once you've done that, ask yourself whether you are living your values day-to-day. If not, what changes will you make as you move *Forward After Fifty?*

In the next chapter, we'll explore how your thinking impacts everything you do.

Chapter 4

MINDSET – YOUR SECRET WEAPON

Y ou can turn fifty and beyond with an outlook that your ancestors could have only dreamt of.

Without a doubt, being able to age healthier for much longer is a game-changer for the whole concept of ageing. Yet, our cultures and predecessors have ingrained our negative expectations of ageing.

To benefit from all that your life has potentially on offer in the 21st century, you may need to shift your mindset (thinking), so in this chapter I will share why this is necessary for not only you but the world economy. We'll be exploring confidence and all that it means, and what might be holding you back.

Building confidence

Being a superpowered woman after fifty requires confidence.

When I think back to situations where I had to make unexpected changes, my low confidence held me back. This lack of confidence was an accumulation of other people's stories and many years of working for other people, fulfilling their values, not mine. If you live authentically, you will be working authentically too.

Starting from scratch in my late fifties had not been on my agenda. I lost confidence, listened to negativity, and I didn't feel worthy. Back then, I was influenced by stories of lost youth, including looks and lively brains. The company I worked for had moved anyway from individualism to focus on brand. Everything and everyone in the company was branded to look and think in the same way. This inflexibility conflicted with my personality and values. Instead of feeling strong with my tools of wisdom, I'd hit a brick wall.

I told myself I needed the experience to become an expert. It didn't occur to me that at fifty-something, I already had a huge amount of experience. So, I began to work on ways to build my confidence. The fantastic thing about confidence is that, like anything, it's something you can develop over time.

I started a journey of self-development, which led to embarking on studying to be a coach. But, unfortunately, my top value of learning became sidelined, and I found myself spending that time in being of service to others, and so I made the excuse of having no time for studies.

I chose to immerse myself in work, instead of learning new things. However, looking back, I realise that all the excuses in the world are not worthy of giving up on personal development.

As I listened to people, I believed that age was not an advantage when it came to change. I bought into these beliefs of others. In fact, what I have learned is the opposite. Age is our very own magical tool.

"I choose what I want to do without worrying about other people so much. Not to be inconsiderate of other people, but not putting them first so often."

Maryna

Wisdom, together with the willingness to be open to learning, is the first step. Forget outdated ageist comments such as "When I was that age, we did that, and it worked". It's time to open your mind and think differently.

Back in the day, we used mental maths to learn our times tables as opposed to calculators, and while that may have made us think differently, that was then, and this is now. Times change.

Open-mindedness allows new ways of thinking and new ideas to be generated, which in turn builds confidence.

The combination of wisdom and the ability to look at new ideas will be empowering. Knowledge, after all, is power and curiosity to absorb the new, and even though it may not always feel comfortable, it will help you build your confidence.

Categorising women as over fifty doesn't allow us to move forward, so we must avoid that old-fashioned viewpoint. It's up to us, as women, to integrate and encourage liberated thinking to have the maximum benefit to ourselves and others.

What Carol, one of my interviewees, initially found was the belief that you can still change your life post fifty. She now has more confidence and believes that you can still go out and get what you want. She believes anything is possible.

She says that "age and experience is priceless". As you get older, "You have the confidence to do things that you wouldn't have done when you were younger".

She went on to say that there can be a period of time where you stop doing things for yourself. She regrets how long it took her to focus back on doing things her way, in the way she wanted to do them. This is a big life lesson. We often do things for others and lose ourselves in the process.

Let's check in on your confidence now:

- How confident are you on a scale of 1-10, where ten is high and one is low?
- What needs to happen for you to feel more confident?

Confidence is situational

Can you be confident in all situations? That's a tall order. It's likely though that you are confident in some areas of your life. For example, you could feel confident that you're a great cook.

Channelling some of that cooking confidence into something else is a great way to build confidence in other areas of your life. Recognising that feeling and applying it to something new can instil confidence in another area.

When you feel confident in an area it's often because you've either learned a skill that makes you believe in your ability, or you have that ability and through evidence have learned that you're good at it.

Discover what you're good at, which may be a hobby, an interest, an activity, a profession, then dive deeper into any of those. You will already have a base to build on.

If you don't know where to start, write down ten things you are already doing and ten things that you'd love to do. Notice the areas you feel confident in and write a list of how you can build your confidence in those areas you want to improve.

I'm going to share an incredible technique with you called Modelling that can help you become the person you want to be.

Fake it – how others 'do' confidence

Building confidence is about keeping negativity out and putting positivity in. The most confident human will not be satisfied in everything they do. Tennis professionals confident in their game may find walking into a press conference an excruciating experience. They're not some superhero. They're human, like you.

You can't be brilliant at everything. You don't need to prove anything, and what's more make sure you're not judging yourself by listening to your inner critic. If you do, you won't even start anything new.

Don't waste time comparing yourself to others, as you are unique. You have your own life experiences.

Let's take networking, which can be intimidating. Going into a room full of people and introducing yourself, well, just thinking about it may be enough to stop you from going. The point is that everyone feels the same. That fear unites the people in the room.

Yes, some will appear more confident, as they've done it before and gone through what you are experiencing. But, the stage is your platform, your performance is the objective, the rehearsal with the script will take many times to get it right.

Modelling is where you take an element of a behaviour that you desire and you emulate it. For example, if you were at a networking meeting, you might notice a person that exudes confidence. You would note a few things about that person's confidence, such as their posture, how they engage with people or something else that stands out.

You then take one of those elements and practise it. The more you practise it, the more confident you will become. You obviously need to do this in your own authentic way. It's a great skill to help you build your confidence.

"My challenge of being over 50 has been to take myself much more seriously, and just put myself out there."

Janice

Overcoming self-doubt

Starting something new often brings self-doubt. There is a consensus that life starts slowing down or even stopping when you're over fifty. It can be challenging to deal with feelings of self-doubt.

"I regret not actually having stood up for myself more, having not actually carved more of a love for myself. To be totally absorbed in somebody else's life is actually not a good thing. I'm forgiving myself for choices that I made that I felt were the wrong ones."

Karen

Here are some helpful tips to keep your self-doubt under control:

- Choose to be in an environment where you are happy with people that make you feel good
- Permit yourself to say NO to what you don't want
- Value your experience/wisdom
- Respect yourself – Self-respect will build your self-confidence, allowing you to be free to choose differently.

New starts after fifty may seem fearful, unpredictable, and uncomfortable at first.

"Please don't listen to other people's stories. Their stories belong to them, not you. Instead, choose to talk to yourself positively. I can; I will, I am."

Source unknown

Be grateful to family and friends who support your reinvention, and if they don't, then that's all good too, because this is your journey. ***After fifty is the time to serve yourself.***

Don't use age as an excuse to stop. On the contrary, your age can be an excuse to start. This is your time to do what you want to do; no one, not even you, needs to stop you.

It is time to share your experiences, the wisdom you've accumulated, the lessons you have learned, your expertise.

RISING REINVENTORS

Not everyone will like you; none of us love everything, so rejection in some areas is natural. But, on the other hand, rejection is protection, so a wise person said. Therefore, trust that it will be for the right reasons if rejection comes your way. Instead, allow other paths to appear.

Here are some strategies to get rid of self-doubt:

- **Surround yourself with the right people:** Be accountable and declare your intentions. Stop people-pleasing, and instead spend time with people who you know appreciate you as you are.
- **Manage your mindset:** Catch your negative self-talk. Change your inner dialogue, so instead of telling yourself, "I can't do this because I've never done it before", instead tell yourself, "I can do this".
- **Reframe your self-doubt:** CHOOSE to take control. Remind yourself it is your life, not anybody else's.
- **Recognise your excuses:** What's going on? Listen to yourself and your excuses, and if it's not something you want to do, don't do it, but if it's something you long to do, take action!
- **Stop looking for validation:** From others, instead, look to yourself. If you have encouragement and admiration from others, acknowledge it.
- **Become an expert:** This needs practice and time, so work on your strengths and what interests you.
- **Expect rejection:** Nobody can please everybody; we have different core values. So, accept that some people will

not want to work or be with you. You will then surround yourself with the right people rather than the wrong.

Worrying prevents you making your life after fifty be some of the best years of your life. It is a negative emotion that does not serve us.

"I don't remember hearing or even talking about anxiety when we were in our twenties", said Kath, my good friend and one of my interviewees for this book. I agreed with her, as I don't think we did worry. Instead, we viewed life as falling into place – having a home, car, career and money. So, no, worrying wasn't on the agenda in our twenties.

There are always going to be people that worry and who are always negative. They will explain their negativity away as their protection. They perhaps believe that worrying enables them to be ready for all possibilities, which for the most part, never appear. Unfortunately, an awful lot of worry energy can often lead to health-related issues.

One of the Oxford dictionary definitions of worry is to feel or cause to feel anxious or troubled about actual or potential problems.

Anxiety is a feeling of worry, nervousness, or unease about something that has an uncertain outcome.

Whether you are anxious or worried about changing your life, you can start controlling some of your worries. Worries shouldn't be boxed up and allowed to simmer inside. Instead, releasing worries and fears by voicing them takes away some of their power. You can often discover that you had no reason to worry in the first place.

An excellent strategy for working through your worries is to write them down on paper. Then add them to a worry journal or box if you want to take this a step further. Finally, write down a potential solution for each of your worries.

If you let your mind ruminate, you can start to spiral.

What other people think about us is a widespread concern. Challenge your thinking. Why does it matter to you so much what other people think?

If spending time with a particular person makes you doubt yourself, then question if you need that person in your life at all. Often though, it's not others. The most critical person judging you in your life is often you.

Judgement can make us feel worried. I know someone who never invited people to dinner or coffee as she worried about what they would think of her house. Due to this worry, she'd be invited to other people's houses on various occasions and never return the invite.

She was too concerned with what people would think of her 'tiny house', her furniture and more. This wasted energy resulted in a lack of connection and social life.

If someone doesn't like your taste, home or your clothes, does it matter in the end? What's important is that you want it. It's how you choose to live. So, which is more important – socialising or worrying about how someone is judging you?

"I feel fabulous! Ageing is an opportunity to be me."

Carol

Create a list of positive actions instead of negative thoughts. There are so many benefits:

- You will feel fabulous and in control
- You will look more attractive
- You will feel less worried and be more carefree.

People-pleasing

I'd never heard of the term 'people pleaser' until I studied coaching at 56 years old; it was one of those lightbulb moments that comes with coaching.

I asked myself whether I had been a people pleaser rather than pleasing myself. The answer is pivoting towards a yes. My education looms in the background: we had to say yes at school as there was a peril to anyone who answered no.

Saying no to parents was also a no-no.

What culture tells a woman to say no? It's no surprise we become people pleasers. Traditionally women were keepers of the home, yet women's lives were transformed following the example in both world wars when they took on male jobs. Thus began the need to work for our independence and financial survival.

Cultures and education never prepared us for this, so we've been left to our own devices. Unlike the transformation of women's roles during the past century, a similar change in men's roles has failed to take place, something the feminist movement has been fighting ever since. Women are still expected to be the primary keepers of the home, and the main bearers of the responsibilities of parenting, while now also developing a demanding career in the workplace. No wonder we're so frazzled!

Now, baby boomers and Generation X are being thrown into the part of their lives, over fifty, where tradition still expects them to slow down and yet continue to keep so many different plates spinning. We are expected to keep pleasing everyone else within the traditional roles set for us. Potentially, the number of roles we are now expected to fulfil even increases. On top of being a partner, parent and worker, we are now expected to be the principal grandparent to the next generation and the main carer to parents or parents-in-law. The extent of people-pleasing can become endless! However, the reality is that life has changed; we haven't aged as expected. It's time to take a stand!

Saying no to children, parents or partners with needs is no easy option. The question you must ask yourself is, can they look after themselves? If your world needs to change, you may have to say no to the people you love.

Are you making excuses to stop yourself from having your own life?

Perhaps you worry you'll be abandoning your grandchildren, children and parents for your pursuits. Don't let other people's judgement get in your way. They want you to stay as you are; it's probably to their advantage.

The highest priority of duty is to yourself. Leading a more interesting and creative life that stretches you to feel more of who you are and what you have to offer will significantly help you to feel happier and more fulfilled. Along with that comes a kinder, more generous and tolerant character. This can only be of great benefit to our relationships with family, friends and all we encounter.

Start delegating

Could you delegate work to others rather than doing everything yourself? How about making compromises with the people you love or creating a plan to suit you.

As women, cleaning, cooking and washing have all been traditional roles. Yet, women did not usually work once married; times have changed. Sometimes it may seem too overwhelming to ask others in the household for help. You may feel you might as well get on with it yourself or even be on a mission to prove you can do it all.

Stop saying sorry!

I have a friend who repeatedly says "Sorry". Do you know someone like that, or does it remind you of yourself? Of course, you don't need to say sorry unless you've done something wrong. It's a British trait to say sorry. For example, when you cross someone accidentally, an unavoidable bumping into someone becomes a polite "Sorry" response.

If you're like me and fall into adopting this trait, listen to yourself and control the 'sorry' word. Taking the blame is disempowering, and we want to use our superpowers, not the opposite.

Speaking words without thinking is something we all do. It's a case of making changes by listening to ourselves. Stop saying yes when you mean no.

Stop asking others for approval. I noticed myself saying to my husband, "Shall I make the fire, or shall I do this/that?" It wasn't a question, more like a habitual sentence; I've changed my language to a statement such as, "I'm making the fire".

Sometimes, telling the truth doesn't suit people-pleasers; it can make you look vulnerable or disagreeable. So, instead, you go along with other people's ideas, even though they may be the last thing you want to do. You have this notion that nobody wants to hear your opinion, you don't count, and it's better to keep quiet as it's easier to go with the flow.

Even when someone compliments you, you're more comfortable not taking the praise and will shift the kind words directed towards you to someone else.

Isn't it time to reward yourself with an Oscar for life authenticity instead of an Oscar for service to everyone else?

- Focus on you, not others; this may be better late than never
- Help people because you want to and not because you feel you must
- Build up your confidence to be a conqueror and a winner
- Notice when you say yes when you mean no. Practise saying no
- Our language becomes our actions. So, stop, listen and change
- Be willing to change to become the person you'd love and respect.

Create boundaries

According to the Oxford dictionary, boundaries are, "a line which marks the limits of an area; a dividing line". So, how can creating boundaries, if you need to, affect life after fifty?

Mel Robbins sums up boundaries:

> **"They define what you are tolerating. If someone crosses over your line, say stop."**

What do you allow, and more importantly, are you communicating what boundaries you have in place? Creating boundaries is all about communication.

Let's say you disagree with how a friend behaves with you; do you say something or nothing? Please don't simply blame the other person for their behaviour, if you haven't said what you want, need or more bluntly, what you don't like or need. I remember a person who was a friend at the time would borrow money left, right, and centre (even from people I'd introduce her to) and then stalled on paying it back. I found this so uncomfortable, yet I didn't communicate my feelings; in the end, I let go of this friendship.

Mel Robbins says you can't change other people, but you can train them how to treat you, and if they continue to step over your boundaries, then it's time to let go.

Again, it's about your feelings, your self-respect. Letting go is freeing.

Over-fifties' women and boundaries

Many of us come weighed down by the culture of serving and people-pleasing. As a result, it simply may not have crossed your mind to think about imposing boundaries – it certainly hadn't crossed mine until my fifties. Is it too late to set some? No, it's never too late to make changes that will contribute to a beautiful life and your reinvention. You can always start something new. However, when it comes to people, boundary setting can be complex.

Have you been in the position of wanting to express your opinion, but your friends or family speak over you, so it's easier not to say anything? Communicating that it's your turn to talk rather than feel frustrated inside will be better for you. It's all too easy to be stuck in these habits:

- We accommodate others before ourselves
- We want to solve other people's problems, including our family and friends
- We stay in relationships that don't serve us
- We don't ask for what we want.

So, boundaries are not always easy to implement: they take courage.

If you're not living your authentic life, now is the time. It's essential to feel healthy and empowered.

Knowing your values will make it easier to set boundaries. Refer back to Chapter 3 for more information.

Setting personal boundaries

I can think of endless occasions, even years, where my boundaries were pretty much near to zero.

I hadn't even heard of boundaries until I studied coaching. Such a powerful tool to have in life. One that would have made a difference in the past, but I'm excited to have it to navigate into my future.

I know someone that pours out her life story whenever I bump into her. She shares both the good and the bad. We don't know each other very well. She is someone who appears to have no boundaries, making herself vulnerable and susceptible to falling victim to judgment as she lets everybody into her private life.

If you know somebody like this, set a boundary for yourself, even if you need to excuse yourself from someone oversharing.

Setting work boundaries

You may be in a job and feel vulnerable because you don't feel overly confident due to your age. On the other hand, you may be starting a new career, making you feel the same. Boundary settings will make you feel stronger. When people know your boundaries, they will respect you for being a superpower woman.

Remember that you are as worthwhile as everybody else, and boundary setting, when new, will take time. Rehearse your script and make sure that everything you do from now on is how you want to live. You can only be yourself, know your limitations and work within your values. If you don't like what you're experiencing, let people know or go.

"I'm slowly learning not to be bothered by what others might think. I don't feel the need to be on show."

Janice

What's holding you back?

The 3 biggest fears

Below are 3 of the biggest fears that came up throughout my interviewee conversations. Do not let fear stop you.

Fear #1 There's not enough time to:
- **Reinvent my life –** Just do it; your age doesn't matter. Now is the time.
- **Activate my wish list –** Go to your list, prioritise your top wish and take a small action step today towards making it happen.
- **Be a grandparent –** You could have a good 30 years plus. If it's meant to happen, it will.

- **Find meaning in life –** You can always find meaning in life. Don't make the idea of a lack of time or an excuse not even to start.
- **Start a new career –** You can learn new skills easily these days to kick-start a new direction.
- **See the world –** There's always time to travel: pick a destination, start some new adventures, and explore.

Fear #2 Weight gain and physical/mental decline

The second biggest fear that came up was around health issues. Most participants mentioned the fear of weight gain and physical/mental decline. Topics such as loss of independence due to bad health and age-related diseases, i.e., dementia, were high on people's lists.

If I were sitting with you, I would be telling you the following:

- Prevention is better than cure
- Exercise, stretch, run, dance, walk, move. Build muscle strength
- Meditate
- Be food conscious, eat well – manage your nutrition
- Focus on your body interior rather than the exterior

- Be accountable to yourself for your health. Stop waiting for ill health to happen. Take your health into your own hands. Learn all you can to improve your wellbeing
- Exercise your brain, i.e., mind exercises, puzzles, crosswords
- There are many ways to improve your wellbeing, especially with everything being easily accessible.

Fear #3 Being alone

As humans, we crave connection. We want to be around people. So, the third biggest fear was around being alone.

Some of the specific fears that came up were:

- Being abandoned
- Loss of friends and family
- No longer being valued
- Feeling vulnerable
- Not being in touch with technology and life changes in the modern world
- Being overly comfortable by yourself that you lose the ability to socialise and connect.

Here are a few ways to overcome these fears:

- Keep connected via social media, meet-ups and phone
- Get involved in the community, join clubs, networking or interest groups; be a committee member to find like-minded people
- Work on your self-development
- Update your skills: do a course, learn a new hobby
- Build your intergenerational network where all ages learn from each other
- Stay independent
- Stay curious
- Explore.

Two other fears that often came up were the fear of failure and the fear of success. Let's explore these in some more depth.

Fear of failure

My education taught me that failure was to be feared, so much so that fear stopped you in your tracks. This prevented me from trying. This is not my blame game. No, it's the reality of working out what it was that stopped me from moving forward.

Fear is an unpleasant emotion caused by the threat of danger, pain or harm. Fear has protected you by keeping you alert for the baddies and wild animals as you run through the dark forest. Still, you're probably not doing that now. Instead, we often deal with anxiety – fear of failure, fear of success, embarrassment, rejection, and the unknown.

Failure, by definition, is a lack of success. Being at the top of your game, being first, being something that you couldn't possibly be in high school. These beliefs could become patterns for your future.

We were taught to be perfectionists on some level. By being a perfectionist, you refuse to accept any standard short of perfection, which is another hurdle that stops you from even trying.

Throw fear of failure together with a dash of perfectionism, and you have the perfect reason to stop yourself from ever wanting to reinvent your life.

RISING REINVENTORS

I certainly had an ingrained fear of failure stopping me from moving on, back when I lost the job I'd come to rely on for finance and all that goes with it – what a wake-up call that had been. Finally, instead of working for other people's values, I could work for mine, albeit it took me some years to appreciate that.

My goal now is to make sure you waste no time discovering how important you are and how doors are open, not closed for you now as you move *Forward After Fifty*.

A quote by entrepreneur Richard Branson: "The best lesson is usually learned from failure". It is a quote to ponder, as every failure is a learning point. The critical part of failure is that you have tried where so many others don't.

Start to shift your thought process to believe that failure is directing you to create something better and that outlook can manoeuvre you into your most successful time.

As a woman over fifty, undoubtedly, you will have experienced rejection. I once had a relationship that I couldn't let go of (I didn't recognise then that one of my core values was challenge). On reflection, I'm grateful for what happened. I feel a guardian angel may have saved me from a bad experience. The point is not to fear rejection; it's a positive, taking you in a better direction.

Fear of success

Fear of success can hold you back. It's strange because, indeed, if success is the goal, you would think we wouldn't want to sabotage it.

Often, we may start to wonder if the pursuit of success means we will have to put in more hours, lose some of our social life and drop other commitments. But, like rejection and failure, words we can now use positively, the fear of disappointment can stop you from trying.

Disappointment – sadness or displeasure caused by the non-fulfilment of one's hopes or expectations. So, is the risk of disappointment a good reason not to have a go at something new or rekindle a project/job? The risk factor is the disappointment of not starting.

I ran a survey a while ago asking what success meant to people. The responses were insightful. It brought over twenty-one different answers, proving success is personal.

Success could mean change, something that women over fifty often contemplate but do not necessarily embrace. But, with wisdom, we can have success on our terms.

There may be an underlying fear that success could upset friends or family.

You cannot let success hold you back. Share your achievements. You never know who you might inspire.

"A positive experience is in being able to help so many people because of everything that you've done."

Carol

I'll do this when...

Do you find yourself saying, "I'll do this when..."? The 'when' is a time factor or a moment in the future that you deem to be the right time.

You know procrastination can keep you safe. But, of course, you can't go wrong if you don't take a risk.

You might tell yourself that when you're older, you will make a particular thing happen. Now you've turned fifty, and you feel ready for a change. You know that the time is right, as you are now well and truly grown up, yet you might begin making excuses because you don't know where to start, which can lead to you blaming others, or yourself, for not having made the decision or taken action earlier.

What to do first is often the problem, which makes you spiral into overwhelm. The knock-on effect of this is that you feel lousy, so much so that you stop.

I've been there so many times throughout my life that, previous to fifty, I just tended to accept the status quo and carried on. I would then wonder why I wasn't feeling how I wanted to feel as I moved on through the years.

Finally, a couple of wake-up calls led to my development journey, where I learned that I had a choice. I could either stay in my corner and play the blame game. Alternatively, I could create a plan.

You might know what you want, you may only need to take that first step, or you may have to rediscover yourself and begin a reinvention.

Don't put life on hold.

As Janice says, "Just get on with it, and stop finding excuses".

Most women over 50 will go through perimenopause and menopause.

This can be a time when it can feel as though you are no longer going to be the person you were, and along with hot flushes, insomnia and brain fog, to name but a few, the fear of ageing can kick in.

I want to offer you a fresh perspective: how about if you looked forward to the positive transitions of menopause rather than resisting them?

RISING REINVENTORS

No more period pain, no premenstrual symptoms, no more tampons/pads, no more birth control. More energy, yes more!

Women's empowerment might reach an all-time high if we were positive concerning menopause!

Guilt

Doing things for others and not for yourself alleviates the uncomfortable emotion of guilt raising its ugly head. However, there is a cost to *you* if this stops you from doing what you want to do.

Would eliminating some people-pleasing habits make you feel guilty? Ask yourself this question – how does feeling guilty make me feel better?

Don't let other people's needs raise feelings of guilt in you because that's the problem – it's their needs, not yours.

"When we reach 50, we can step forward in power to tap into our passion, and not become somebody else's pocket."

Janine

Assess regret and disappointment

I've frequently heard the words 'regrets' and 'disappointment' in conversations with my interviewees for this book. The underlying message of these words is, "If only I'd done this or that before fifty".

Are regrets and disappointment the same?

So, thinking about regret:

- The verb: feel sad, repentant, or disappointed over (something that one has done or failed to do)
- The noun: a feeling of sadness, repentance, or disappointment over an occurrence or something that one has done or failed to do.

When asked what my regrets are, I used to say that I regretted not pursuing attending drama school. As an 18-year-old, I tried, and I did have a place, yet the finance question came up, preventing me from pursuing that dream. I now understand that it wasn't my path. Nowadays, I view anything that I failed to do as a positive.

I suspect my mother may have regretted marrying my father after a whirlwind romance lasting six weeks, which finally ended in an acrimonious divorce. However, her regret was my fortune. I was born. I could regret wasting time in my youth; it's regrettable to lose time. I've chosen, albeit better later than never, to ensure that that particular regret means I don't waste any time now.

Two of my interviewees explained that their vision of post-fifties family bliss had been shattered by marriage break-ups causing great disappointment. Instead, they had been unexpectedly thrown onto different paths and feeling positive was the last thing on their mind.

Expecting something that doesn't work out makes you prone to disappointment. Cultures create expectations, especially when it comes to relationships and families. I don't believe anyone escapes. We can have an illusion of what a parent is meant to be, and they often don't live up to our expectations. Because of this illusion, I could accept some of my father's behaviours.

As Karen said to me, "If my marriage hadn't finished, I wouldn't have had half the experiences that this particular period of freedom allowed me to have over fifty".

If your regrets and disappointments hang heavily, look at this cut-off point of being an experienced over-fifty woman as an opportunity to reinvent your life. Although it may feel challenging, when you view mistakes as positives that keep you off the wrong path and redirect you to a different one, life is more straightforward.

CHAPTER REFLECTION

In this chapter, I've shared some top tips with you. Here are 3 tips to get you thinking:

- Choose to believe that life doesn't stop as you age. You have a lot to offer the world.
- You can choose to let go of negativity around ageing. Make the decision today to age positively.
- Worrying will not promote longevity or happiness. If worry is impeding you from moving *Forward After Fifty*, it's time to confront these worries.

TAKE ACTION

It's easy for your mind to spiral out of control as you tell yourself a destructive story about ageing. How different would life be for you if you had a new self-belief that life is only just beginning as you move *Forward After Fifty*?

Pick one negative thought you want to eliminate from your life and create a plan to make that happen. Review your progress after one week. i.e.:

Thought: *I regret that I didn't leave the relationship with … sooner.*

Plan: *When this thought comes up, I will remind myself that I took action as soon as I realised it wasn't working.*

In the next chapter, we will concentrate on your health and wellbeing, as it is vital that you take control of this instead of waiting for infirmity.

Chapter 5

WELLBEING IN YOUR HANDS

After being moulded by society into a category of 'older' beings that wait for the inevitable to happen, such as bad health, impaired mobility, mental anxiety, loneliness, and weight gain, it's no wonder that nobody wants to age or even think about ageing.

The good news is that you are living in a world where there are so many new ways to look after your wellbeing. Being healthy isn't a quick fix, not at all; instead, it's all about you making an effort, and in this chapter, you'll learn how.

I don't feel spiritual wellbeing needs to be awkward. Many people simply assume spirituality is purely religious. It may be for many, but it can also be so much more – a sense of connection to something bigger than ourselves; a place we can carve out within us where we recognise the beauty of life on our planet; and the awe and wonder we can experience when we consciously stop and take a minute to experience something magical like a glorious sunset. It can be deeply rewarding and uplifting to step out of our overactive minds for a minute or two and look around us at the rest of creation, and just marvel.

Wellbeing is in your hands.

Acceptance vs resistance

During my research for this book, everyone mentioned health. I've had many conversations with women who look at ageing going hand in hand with bad health. Age can mean different things depending on the cultural view. Take Japan for example. Ageing is positive. The older generation is often revered for their wisdom.

The reality is that nobody wants poor health. Nobody wants to age.

When I questioned a doctor as to why I had contracted breast cancer, his response was, "You're over fifty," which I didn't think was particularly helpful.

How would you feel if you chose not to accept that your future is filled with health issues because "you're over fifty"? You are living in a time when you have the knowledge and the tools to do your best to prevent health problems.

Undoubtedly, ageing healthily wouldn't go down very well with the enormous profit-making businesses in the anti-age sector. However, what you might not be aware of is that pro-age businesses are rapidly replacing this.

Forbes business magazine suggests ageing adults are not only consumers, they are our only increasing natural resource; a talent pool that can power businesses and enhance future communities. And they are ready, willing and able to be deployed.

Physical wellbeing

Weight gain

Weight gain is a general concern and, for many, a reality after fifty. Being body-conscious reaches a new level: why? Many of us have been telling ourselves we're going to put on weight. We might say things like:

- "It's inevitable due to hormone changes."
- "I'm going to lose control of my body."
- "My body shape will change due to hormones."

We almost allow the weight to reach us. It's as if it's expected. So, unfortunately, you may have read more about weight gain than keeping the extra pounds off.

Understand your body

While this book is not dwelling on the menopause it would be remiss of me not to mention it at some point, particularly where you may experience symptoms as you move *Forward After Fifty*.

While menopausal police will be telling you the doom and gloom story, you are in the advantageous position of being able to acquire knowledge to help you prepare for this time of life if the symptoms arrive. You can make physical and mental preparations to look after your body.

Everyone's menopause journey is individual to them. Mine was a relatively easy one. I chose to take a herbal remedy to keep me mentally balanced. Yes, I could allow more weight to go on or choose to release some weight. I lost ten kilos as a result. However, keeping it off has been a work in progress. I've tried to spend more time understanding my body instead of comparing it to everyone else's.

What does your body need? A healthy nutritional plan and a regime of kindness and care so you feel happy and healthy, physically and mentally. This time in your life is meant to be lighter, your happy time. It is also the most crucial time to take care of yourself.

Prevention is always better than cure, and even if you have not spent much time looking after yourself, you can start today.

For example, did you know that one in three women over fifty will have a problem with their bones due to a lack of the priceless mineral calcium? Yet this is so easy to improve. Add more dairy, leafy vegetables and nuts/seeds into your day.

I am not qualified in nutrition, so check out my podcast interview with Lisa Plutoni over on my website, who shares lots of ways that we can use our foods as preventative tools and age healthily.

Healthy Lifestyle Over Fifty Podcast
https://apple.co/3G54duk

"It's all in the head. It's all about mindset. That's it. If you eat healthily, and your mind is healthy, and your body is healthy, it's not a problem. You can age gracefully."

Lisa

Wellbeing is so much more important than wrinkles. Where possible, take action to prevent some illnesses that can be a result of your lifestyle choices. You can't prevent wrinkles, so it's undoubtedly better to do what you can do, rather than what you can't!

Protect your sleep

I'm not a night owl; my energy belongs to the mornings; sleep is essential. Are you protecting your sleep pattern? Superpowered women like us need to recharge. Sleep is our healing, and anything you take on that requires extra energy needs a sleep boundary. So, wind down pre-sleep and do whatever it takes to have your protected sleep hours.

Movement/exercise

Movement/exercise is non-negotiable for me, which is in two daily walks and Pilates reformer classes. My boundaries are around my schedule, which I must do to keep my health, meaning my mental and physical welfare.

Are you keeping your car in good working order, serviced regularly, oiled and watered? If not, the consequence is usually a breakdown, particularly if it's an older model. We can apply the same principle to ourselves, as we need the same care inside and out. In addition, exercise has been proven without doubt to extend our lives healthily.

Whatever type of movement you do already, keep doing it. Don't make age an excuse to stop you from moving; it's an excuse to start. Research tells us that it isn't a problem to begin if you've never exercised and you can build muscle at any age. There are many ways to exercise. Find a movement/exercise that you enjoy. That way you're more likely to stick with it long-term.

I love the story of *Train with Joan* who I mentioned earlier and can be found on Instagram. She is, I believe, a true influencer in every sense of the word. She proves that whatever you have to start with, movement/exercise can be a lifesaver. She's a woman who has transformed her body from the age of 70 into a picture of health at 75.

It's time to change that negative mindset that tells you it's not worth the effort. Ditch the excuses. You don't need to cover up. Instead of thinking 'beautiful' bodies, think 'healthy' ones. Feeling a little achy from a workout is one hundred times better than living with aches with pains.

"We as women definitely need to eat well to live well. And because, you know, what are we without health?"

Carol

My top tips for physical wellness

- *Hydrate, hydrate, hydrate.* Drink more water.
- *Improve your nutrition.* Today, you have no excuse not to learn the basics of creating preventative methods for your overall health.
- *Keep moving!* Find some form of movement that you enjoy.

Emotional wellbeing

Letting go

Another client I interviewed explained that on reaching her fifties, it was time to let go of partners' and children's (now adults') emotions. Their emotions physically drained her and emotionally distracted her, so much so that her ambitions were being sidelined. So, she chose to believe it was time to live life on her terms.

RISING REINVENTORS

Concern for our family and friends is normal; nevertheless, decisions need to be made when their issues take your precious energy. Are you living your life now for you or them? Choosing to live life on your terms might come across as selfish, but as my client said to herself, this is your time now. What makes you happy isn't selfish; it's vital.

As a child, I can clearly remember my parents arguing and, being so young, me taking on their emotions. I recall feeling quite sick at the time, where I was being catapulted into the grown-up world too early.

Encounters of all sorts enrich life, both negative and positive. Sharing our encounters with others helps us either spread joy or allows us to find support when things go wrong.

When we become entangled in the emotions of others, however, we can start to forget our life journey, and that can come at a considerable cost.

"Being able to do my own thing and gaining the maturity and understanding that I am my person and don't have to play small anymore."

Janine

Set boundaries

Boundaries and the ability to say no at the right time are your life-savers.

Investing in other people when it's time to let go can be painful.

Many mothers I've spoken to mention that the space left by children is hard to fill. Adjustment to this new period can even be traumatic. Yet, some people embrace their newfound freedom. I remember one of my friends saying she couldn't wait to spend time with her partner again and start rediscovering their relationship.

A client spoke to me about the learning process of discovering the advantages of serving herself. She said that it was sometimes more difficult for the rest of the family to accept that she would fill this new space and time with her dreams, business and pursuits. She was no longer happy to play small. While it was difficult for everybody around her in the early stages, she said the pain was worth it.

She went on to say, "Choosing to be independent rather than dependent has given me the freedom of choice". If one of your core values is freedom, you may be feeling extremely driven, which keeps you motivated to achieve your goals.

Don't lose sight of yourself in relationships or even lose yourself at all.

I hear clients say, "I'm hopelessly in love". I wonder if perhaps it's best never to feel hopeless, even if it's in love.

Take yourself seriously

We can spend time reasoning why not to do something; it's easier to stay put. But, all the same, that's your loss and mine because what you share will benefit others.

Do you think you've got what it takes? If you don't believe you have, then this can be a challenge if you're not taken seriously as a strong and independent woman over fifty.

Test yourself by entering a room with a group of men and women of mixed ages. You can't identify who's in charge straightaway, but you need to speak to the leader. I wonder who you will move to first, the little older woman at the far end of the room? You might do if her name was Queen Elizabeth.

Positivity

Positivity is empowering and a choice. Therefore, I choose to surround myself with positivity.

If you were asked to write ten positive facts about ageing, what would they be? Here are some of my positive statements that you can also use as mantras:

- I have experiences to share
- I know what's good for me
- I follow my instincts with confidence
- I no longer worry about what other people think of me
- I embrace ageing
- I no longer use negative expressions to describe myself
- I make decisions that empower my journey
- I can learn from each challenge I face and overcome
- I now have time for myself
- I feel free.

"I never looked after myself. I looked after everybody else and I completely and totally forgot about myself."

Colette

Mental wellbeing

Respect yourself and your decisions

Being so preoccupied with other people's needs to the extreme that your needs are put aside is counter-productive for wellbeing. Deciding to put yourself first can feel uncomfortable and even evoke feelings of guilt as you can begin to enjoy a new sense of freedom. Guilt is an emotion that won't serve you. It will only hold you back.

You *can* change direction. However, your friends and family may try and talk you out of it because it doesn't suit them. They are used to you behaving in a certain way, so it can be uncomfortable for them when you change. Your change can even trigger some people to recognise changes they want to make but haven't.

One client said that starting a business meant sacrificing time usually spent looking after her family's needs. Naturally, this led to her having to have some difficult conversations. However, she was determined to stay on track. Now that her self-respect and decisiveness have paid off, she reaps success and shares her skills with people who need them.

Find time to relax

One of the many myths of being over fifty is that there will be plenty of time to relax. On the contrary, a common complaint of the over-fifties is that they notice that energy levels drop and that they have more than ever to do. You will often hear retirees saying they have no idea how they had time to hold down a job.

I often wonder whether lack of energy is due to doing more than previously. Perhaps the change is that you are starting to do everything you've always wanted to do, making it even more important to take time to relax. Being still in your favourite environment, whether in a cosy armchair or walking in nature, is of the utmost importance.

Many women, as indeed myself, feel an even bigger affinity with nature, whether it's colours, sounds, fauna, the feel of the wind or rain.

Retirement in the past may have been associated with time to relax. Most women I've spoken to say that their lives start to be busier after fifty. So, utilising time smartly to include quiet periods becomes even more critical.

Social media

If you've just embraced it now, you're going to need to restrict this time-zapping drainer. The usual is to go onto a social media platform for something specific, and a few minutes later, you've noticed how many other paths you've gone down. Then you forget why you were there in the first place. Be strict and set personal boundaries for yourself to protect your time.

"It was also learning to say no, thank you."

Karen

Protect your brainpower

Unfortunately, too much emphasis on our brains degenerating can have us believe it's a certainty as we age. Yet, there's plenty of research in preventative behaviour that you can improve your brain right now, as well as proof that ageing brains can absorb and retain new information.

Age is not an excuse to expect memory loss; instead, it's an excuse to prevent it.

Health care for our brainpower includes the following:

- Eating food that nourishes the brain
- Exercises to keep your brain strong
- Sleep to heal and re-energise
- Water to hydrate, eliminate toxins and keep us alert
- Meditation to relax
- Switching off technology and winding down before bedtime rather than winding up
- Reading, puzzles, word and card games.

Spend some time using the tools we have to hand to prevent slipping into memory loss. There are some useful apps to improve your brainpower too.

Check out Jim Kwik's podcast show, *Kwik Brain*, which shares lots of tips to keep your brain in good health.

Spiritual wellbeing

The word 'spiritual' can conjure up mixed feelings in people, including myself. Whether you believe in God, the Universe, source, spirit, nature etc, doesn't matter. It's just about how you connect with something bigger than yourself. Perhaps simply loving yourself is the best place to start.

Self-love is self-care

If we love ourselves just a fraction more, I'm convinced we'd sail through life with less stress and attract more goodness into many areas of our lives. Self-love is an integral part of our self-care. Yet self-love conjures up a narcissistic ogre. The dictionary definition of narcissistic is 'having or showing an excessive interest in or admiration of oneself and one's physical appearance'.

Self-love is a regard for one's wellbeing and happiness. *Psychology Today* describes self-love as this: 'If you are happy with yourself and have self-respect, this will, in turn, attract happiness and respect into your life'.

"Finding out that I quite like myself and getting to know myself. I've decided to be a bit kinder to myself."

Colette

Louise Hay, a motivational author, taught the self-care practice of looking into the mirror and appreciating yourself. It's time to start a new relationship with yourself, even if it does feel uncomfortable.

Self-reflection is vital

Fear of failure can stop us from trying anything, and all of us have failed at something. If we're over fifty, it's inevitable. Reflecting on failures can convince us that we went through a difficult patch and emerged more robust on the other side. We need to fail, to keep ourselves off the wrong path. Choosing to think of past mistakes positively enables us to change if we want to.

Have you longed to write, paint or create something but time and other factors have stopped you? I've met many women who have become entrepreneurs or made significant changes over-fifty due to these factors. Statistically, the most successful age group of new businesses are the over-fifties. They are risk-takers with bucket loads of wisdom to share.

Connection and community

Loneliness and being alone are different. Loneliness can be experienced in a room of one hundred people. However, alone, we are by ourselves.

Many of the women I spoke to about ageing voiced concern about loneliness and being alone. But, to prevent ageing from becoming a difficult stage in life, now is the time to do something about it, not when you find yourself already there.

Living in the age of computers has given us a lifeline. Whatever one says about social media, the ability to connect with groups and family far away from where you live is at least one way to prevent feeling lonely.

Living in a foreign country where the culture and language are not my own has been a lesson in conquering loneliness or being alone, no matter what my age. The truth is you need to make a concerted effort to connect with people. It's easy to flippantly say that your troubles will be over if you learn the native language of where you live.

However, that's not true. People are going on with their busy daily lives, which may not include you. Yes, language allows you to join various clubs on offer but building deeper connections takes time. It doesn't happen overnight, no matter how fluent you are.

Expats in any country tend to drift towards people who speak their language. Expats pro-actively seek out opportunities that they wouldn't entertain in their home territory.

There is a mentality of seeking connection to avoid being alone. The same can apply to anything. We tend to seek out like-minded people.

Although pushing ourselves to connect with others can be very uncomfortable to practice, it's a fantastic way to learn new things, meet people who think as you do and stretch your thinking.

When I couldn't find a local networking group that met my business needs, I created one. As a result, I now run a very successful networking group for women.

While some would tell you they feel apprehensive about meeting new faces and introducing themselves, they will also share that the group is a recipe for happiness and creative connections.

Being part of a community feels worthwhile, and if you cannot find one that suits you, make your own! You don't have to be a follower. You can be the leader and the connector. Is there something missing in your community? Don't complain that there's no place/social event to go to. Create it yourself!

If you feel lonely, it could be you're not living your values.

For example, if nature is one of your values and you live in a city, perhaps now is the time to explore different locations that you could move to. Searching for somewhere that makes you feel close to nature could be life-changing.

If you feel lonely because you have no friends in the vicinity, there are so many ways to stay connected – phone, video call, email, WhatsApp etc.

You could also expand your life to help others in your community, offering to contact people who might also feel lonely. You may find helping others with the same problem becomes a solution for you both.

The choices we have today did not exist in the past, i.e., the many ways you can exercise, access to information to improve your mind and body, such as eating better, and practising self-care. Increasingly, we have more opportunities to take control of our health issues than our past generations. Health was viewed differently then.

I look at the body as a machine. Let's use the car as an example; you are likely to have it serviced, give it a shine and do what you can to keep it reliable. A lot of preventative work goes into looking after machinery. There isn't a quick fix. Vehicles need a level of maintenance. Likewise, your body needs the same measures. Wear and tear happen; we're not robots; we're far more complex.

Are you expecting a quick fix?

Is this in line with healthy ageing, or can you put yourself in the driver's seat and take back control?

Prevention is better than cure, and if you don't want to end up like a poorly looked after car, bashed, and frequently breaking down, then start looking after your wellbeing now.

We are only human; therefore, we experience illness. Yes, some will be age-related, but we are more equipped than ever to try and prevent illness when we choose to look after ourselves.

The future looks exciting, as scientists like Dr David Sinclair explore more possibilities of ending age-related diseases, which will mean living a healthier, longer and more productive life. So, check out *Lifespan* by Dr David Sinclair. It has completely changed the way I think about age-related diseases.

Scientists' research has shown that it will be in the not-too-distant future when having an active and healthy life over a hundred won't be unusual.

Apart from taking cutting-edge medications being developed, factors such as taking supplements, regular exercise, correct nutrition and cultivating connectivity will all have their part to play. So, until the science is officially accepted, at least four out of five of these options are available *now* to extend your healthy life.

CHAPTER REFLECTION

In this chapter, you've learned how your wellbeing is in your hands. Here are my 3 top tips to improve your wellbeing.

1. Start paying as much, if not more, attention to your interior self rather than your exterior.
2. Live your life on your terms – stop people-pleasing.
3. Choose what makes you happy. It's not selfish. It's vital.

TAKE ACTION

What changes can you make to your health and wellbeing now that your future self will thank you for?

- Create a list of potential ways to incrementally improve your health and wellbeing.
- Commit to improving one area from your list in the next month.

Some changes might make you feel uncomfortable, but they are empowering. Wellbeing changes are worth investing your time in to feel empowered as you move *Forward After Fifty*.

In Part II, we'll explore how you can reinvent yourself, starting with all things career, both working for yourself or someone else.

Download my free workbooks:

The Secret to Ageing Positively
[rebeccaronane.com/the-secret-to-ageing-positively/],

Forward After Fifty Workbook
[rebeccaronane.com/faf-50-workbook/]

Part Two

INTRODUCTION

In Part 2, we will explore how you can reinvent yourself by reviewing your work, time and independence.

In Chapter 6, *Career Reboot*, we will discuss how you can reboot your career if you choose to.

In Chapter 7, *Time & Curiosity*, you will learn how you can take back control of your time and use your curiosity to add more depth to your life.

In Chapter 8, *Wise New Owl*, I will encourage you to tap into your wisdom, and you'll learn how to believe in yourself more.

In Chapter 9, *Independent Woman*, you will learn how to move away from feelings of vulnerability and step into your power to create a future where you are more self-reliant.

In Chapter 10, *The Power of Gratitude and Forgiveness*, we explore new ways of being that can bring more freedom into your life.

Finally, in Chapter 12, *Your Future Self*, I encourage you to remove all limiting thoughts and beliefs to become a Rising Reinventor!

Chapter 6

CAREER REBOOT

Retirement is a thing of the past.

Let's embrace this new era as we finally move towards women being the boss of their own lives.

 **RISING REINVENTORS**

If you're a boomer like me, running your own company may have simply never entered your mind, and here we are today with the fantastic option of reinventing our life in the workspace, both employed and self-employed. In this chapter, we will explore how you can reboot and or redefine your career, be your own boss, and start something new.

Today's older adults seek meaning and purpose by disrupting retirement norms and expressing increasing interest in lifelong work and volunteering. However, an article in nextavenue.org says that this will only happen if people like you and me recognise our worth, meaning instead of falling into the ageism trap, we step up and become proactive.

The boomers and Generation x have been riding life through many transitions; let's equally embrace this one too.

"I think it's about having more of a global approach to life. Philosophical wisdom. The old wise owl. You have a certain experience so you can put things in perspective."

Lisa

I started writing this book in 2021 when working had changed dramatically. Buying a house no longer depends on how many bedrooms but how many studies/offices are available. Working from home has gone from a possibility to normality. We are living in a prime period to start our businesses from home.

If you have physical disabilities or envisage something in your future, you can create the perfect environment to move and work in. We have lived a lifetime of unprecedented changes which have made our lives easier and more comfortable, so what lies ahead will be exciting.

In January 2020, flying from London to Marseilles, I read an article in a BA magazine about the potential help for people who may be isolated or unable to look after themselves by robots and drones. Even though this may sound alarming, it means the independence of people in the future is looking much better than today.

Ageing has been dominated, from the mid-20th century onwards, by the concept of retirement, which means mainly stopping work and, in an ideal world, doing what we want with our savings.

Take someone my age born in a generation where men retired at 65 and women at 60. Women didn't expect to be creating businesses or sometimes even working beyond marriage. We changed, we adapted, and we are continuing to do so.

Work was a job for life and often meant doing something you didn't care for, yet changing jobs gave the impression of not being reliable.

Today, if you remain in the same position longer than four years, it's considered strange. How times change.

"The challenging part is adapting to an ageing body when you don't feel older. In my mind, I am a young, dynamic woman."

Carol

Following YOUR dreams

Did you have a dream that was shattered back at school by the careers officer? Unfortunately, you're not on your own.

During my research, I had an interview with Maxine. She shared the following story about her careers officer:

Maxine: "I want to be an actress."

Careers officer: [*Laughing*] "Shall we put you down as going for a job in the local department store as a salesperson then?"

Maxine: Left the room, slamming the door behind her.

How many of us would have been brave enough to storm out of that office? Certainly not me. People would have viewed saying no to an authority figure as being disrespectful. That was not the done thing.

You are at a time in your life where you are the boss of your destination. If you take control of your life, nothing can stop you, whether you desire to fulfil the dream of a project, lifestyle or a career change.

Many of the women I interviewed for this book sensed the time factor of ageing, and what is now possible played a crucial role in how they are navigating the second half of their lives. It is now or never.

If life had thrown up some regrets, the drive not to have any more regrets has more pull than living the life others think you should lead.

"I was burnt out when I hit 50 because I had a very demanding life."

Karen

We can choose to view life in different ways at that crunch point, either positively, where you choose a better course, or negatively, where you simply believe you're on your last legs.

Career change

During my research a universal response was desiring a change of profession, a change of view. A feeling of wanting to change somehow.

When considering a career change, there are many factors involved.

The most important factor is that you feel fulfilled. Consider your current work and where you're feeling fulfilled, and what you're looking for in a new career. Take into account work/life balance, and the level of reward that you need.

Often as we get older, we change in our need for recognition and validation – we just want a job that lights us up. Reflect on how important it is for you to be recognised for what you do. You will have achieved a great many things over your lifetime, learned skills, gained wisdom, made mistakes and learned from them. You may find that a lot of your skills are transferrable to other work, and if not then you can just update your skills as part of your reinvention.

You may find that your ambition has changed. Perhaps you're not interested in climbing the career ladder. You may even already be at the top of the ladder, but you're not feeling fulfilled and you want a new challenge now.

Have you considered working for yourself? I never had, but I'm now 10 years in at the time of writing, and it's been the most exciting time of my life.

When you think about your current career, spend some time reflecting on how well it suits you, and if it doesn't then consider what you'd like to create instead. There will always be many options available to you, whether it's expanding your current role, up-skilling, or even leaving to start up your own business or something new.

Often, being your own boss is little more than a pipe dream rather than something that people action. So, let's explore how that pipe dream could turn to reality.

RISING REINVENTORS

Being your own boss

If, like me, you've been educated by a generation where women did not run a business, you may not have dared to dream or even think of it as an option. Likewise, I had no idea it was achievable until my late fifties.

My coaching studies led me to join several large groups of women online, where most of the women were creating their businesses. I'm not going to lie, most women were much younger than me, but that didn't stop me. Rather than contemplating "Why me?", I thought, "Why not me?"! I was inspired to embark on it as an exciting journey. As you know, you might be a little more in years to the outside world, but in your head, you're still younger than your actual age. In your world, nothing has changed.

If you want to be your own boss, be the director of your life right now. Below I share some tips to get you started.

What can you offer?

Spend some time going through your skills and experience, work and life. Then, list your superpower(s).

For example, you might find writing easy, yet other people tell you it's really challenging. Because you find it so easy to do, you don't appreciate it's your superpower. If you're not sure what your superpowers are, ask your friends to tell you what they think.

Brainstorm some business ideas that excite you. Then, get all your ideas out of your head and written down on paper. Anything and everything is possible at this stage.

Do some market research around your idea. Your idea needs to be profitable, or you will have an expensive hobby. Ask others for their input to assess its validity.

Identify the problem you solve

Who needs your help? List the kind of people you can and want to help. Describe them in as much detail as possible. What support do they need from you?

Start connecting with people – business groups, local groups, on and/or offline. Talk with other business owners, find out how they got started. Ask what pitfalls and challenges they've faced and how they've overcome them.

People want to listen to your perspective. You are unique and deserve to be heard.

Inspiration

I had no intention of setting up a business, but as I met people in the personal development world after studying coaching, I was inspired to do the same. I joined online groups and as I learned about other women's entrepreneurial journeys, I decided to start up a business of my own.

Consider what/who inspires you

Often, we can't put into words what we desire/want to create. An excellent way to get clearer on this is to notice when people say something that makes you wish you had that too, i.e., when I heard people talking about running their own business, it excited me. I recognised my desire to create something similar for myself.

Back to boundaries

Being your own boss can seem daunting. You might worry about the opinions of family members and the potential judgement of your dreams. If this resonates, read the section on boundaries for more guidance in this area.

Work/life balance

If you were born in the fifties like me, this work/life balance stuff was unheard of. I just started working to have all the necessities. I didn't want to be a nurse, teacher, secretary or housewife, most likely the four paths women in Britain were expected to follow at that time. So work was work and balance was not an option.

Women presumed they wouldn't be working beyond a certain age if they lived in Britain during the seventies/eighties. We'd retire back then at sixty, and that seemed a lifetime away at the time. Then you'd probably live some years with your feet up, followed by the inevitable. Yet the reality is not that at all – turning fifty in the 21st century, your life expectancy could be thirty years plus.

Money continues to be the big issue, because you need a fair amount to live comfortably, therefore back to work but with balance.

I live in France, where retirement remains a hot subject. My impression is that the purpose of work is to pay for the 'Joie de Vivre.' Work hard then play hard.

Not long ago, a particular strike in France featured students angry about the changes to the pensionable age. I cannot ever remember thinking about pensions until now in my sixties, which shows an insight into my money story.

Americans are work-driven with few if not any benefits. Retirement, I suspect, looks like the time for a well-earned rest. However, their work ethic is taking them leaps and bounds ahead of everyone else as the over-seventies create more businesses than ever before. So, we may be watching with curiosity and admiration once again as the US shows how they handle the ageing population.

Your culture can make a difference in how you perceive age; nevertheless, we live in an age where longevity will impact all our lives. For example, financially, the way we learn, intergenerationally, and so much more.

Working on your terms could mean you consider creating something entirely new – a reinvention.

Remember, your experience is a superpower.

RISING REINVENTORS

If you're over fifty now, you may still have children at home, whether adult or young, or be in the role of carer for an elderly parent or friend, perhaps even be a grandparent helping out while your children go to work. Life's responsibilities don't disappear with age, particularly your responsibility to yourself. Therefore, it's important to create balance in your life.

Work/life balance means different things to different people.

Here's what a few of my clients have said:

- "You are managing your time effectively, so you have more freedom."
- "Actively taking care of your health and avoiding burnout through overworking."
- "Making time to exercise so that you are moving." Side note: try not to live a sedentary lifestyle because lack of movement is becoming as dangerous as smoking.

Volunteering

You may be at the point that you no longer want to do 'professional work', be it employed or self-employed. Perhaps you want to free up some time to get involved in your community.

You may want to help out, learn new skills and connect with others. Volunteering can be very rewarding. Whether you have limited or lots of time, you will be able to find something that is a good fit for you.

If professional work no longer excites you, consider how you might get involved in your local community to give your life more meaning and purpose. Remember, the Blue Zone longevity recipe included connection with others.

Creating a better work/life balance

- Refine your work processes – make your tasks easier and/or quicker. It will take time to review how you currently work – however, it will be rewarding once you do.
- Set clear boundaries (and stick to them).
- Create an overall task list and prioritise your top 3 most important tasks.
- Reflect on work done. Note what worked and what didn't work and adapt where necessary.
- Create a 'Do less/Do more' list. On one side of a sheet of paper make a list of all the things that you would like to do less of, and on the other side another list of all the items you'd like to do more of. Review your list and take action.
- Make time to play (the key bit there is to *make* the time!).

It's worth considering your contribution to over-working. For example, you might have a dictatorial boss leaning over your shoulder, or you might be the one that's issuing the orders to yourself.

CHAPTER REFLECTION

1. Are you in your dream career? If not, what needs to change?
2. Could being your own boss be an option?
3. Are you achieving a good work/life balance?

"Work is a rubber ball. If you drop it, it will bounce back. The other four balls, family, health, friends, integrity, are made of glass. If you drop one of these, it will be irrevocably scuffed, nicked, perhaps even shattered."

Gary Keller – *The One Thing*

If you have your dream career or business, that's fantastic news. But, if not, what's stopping you from rebooting or starting a new career to move *Forward After Fifty*?

TAKE ACTION

Is it time to step out of your comfort zone and do something different? If yes, do the following:

- Brainstorm options for your next career move. Don't limit your thinking. Just write whatever comes up for you. You can shortlist your options later. But, for now, let your creativity run wild.
- Next, taking each option in turn, reflect on how it makes you feel.
- Finally, choose one option to explore further.

In the next chapter, we're going to explore time and curiosity. Time – we talk about it constantly – how it's flying by, that there is never enough of it, the post-50 'if only I'd started ten years ago'. There is so much panic around time.

Staying curious is a great way to enhance your life.

Chapter 7

TIME AND CURIOSITY

In this chapter, we'll delve into how you can take control of your time and how to stop underestimating your brain capacity as you age.

The perception of time

What is it with time?

During my research into this fascinating area, it became clear that we all tend to feel that time races away from us the older we become. There is no consensus on why this happens, but plenty of theories – mostly hard to understand sentences, a lot of physics, explanations about slowed-down neural transmitters, and so much more. The view that spoke to me said time went quicker when occupied. But equally, we may have forgotten those times in the past when we were on the time treadmill when we were much younger.

When I reflect on this, I remember feeling bored when I was younger, yearning that the next day might bring change. But I wasn't doing what I wanted to do. I wasn't occupied then, whereas today, I'm so passionate about life that it often feels like I don't have enough time to do everything that I want to do.

What is your perception of time? Maybe you feel as if it's rushing by. Perhaps it feels incredibly slow. Your perception of time will make a massive difference to how you think and feel about ageing.

Now is the right time

If you're not convinced that you can open new doors after fifty, I'd strongly recommend discovering your core values to understand how to move forward on your terms. The difference I found in knowing a little more as to what made me function was like having a veil lifted from my face.

It is so important to live in the now. You are not forgetting about the past but respecting it. So, once more, check your top core values to understand what might have gone wrong and how to avoid further disruption if you can.

Karen was frustrated and assumed she had wasted time pre-fifty. But, she said, "I still have so much to do. And there are things that I'm only doing now that I wish I'd have done much earlier".

My response was, "Would you have been ready to have done those things sooner? Or do you think that age and experience has helped you to do them now?"

Perhaps being on the other side of fifty is not the catch-up time but the *right* time to do what you want. You start to shift and see your life differently; yes, the long road is shorter, which is positive as you need to stop overthinking and get on with what you want to do.

Most of us could easily live another thirty to forty years; that's a lot of the right time to do something fabulous. And what's more, you are different. You're oozing with experience and wisdom. So, take the bull by the horns, as it's the right time now.

The value of age is priceless. What have you got to lose? A lot, so don't stop, start!

If you had forever, what would you do?

This is from my conversation with Karen:

"Age and experience are priceless. When you get to a certain age, something inside you gives you the confidence to do things that you wouldn't have done when you were younger. But there was a time in my life where I stopped doing things for myself, and I regret how long it took me to get the focus back on doing things my way, you know, doing something that I want to do."

While we've already covered regret, Karen's statement reminds us that when you think you have forever, things take forever. When you don't have forever, you're more likely to do something.

Ask yourself the question, "If I was given forever to do a project, what would I do?" Conversely, ask yourself, "If I had only a few weeks to do it, then what would happen?"

"*I wish that I sometimes had more energy. There is a part of me that thinks I wish I had just started things earlier, because I have less years in my life now. I still have so much to do. And there's things that I'm only doing now that I wish I'd have done much earlier.*"

Carol

Make the most of time – it's precious

The fact that we are fifty or over is the perfect time to practise gratitude, to be grateful for everything that has happened in your life so far. Hence, I have no time for anyone who knocks age. A wrinkle is an imprint of the gift of time. The time you have now is the time to give yourself a break or to rediscover so much more. One life is not enough to do everything on offer in the world, whether that's knowledge, travel, connection, and creation. Time to think about what you are going to do, then time to do it. What's stopping you? Not time.

Because time is so precious, if you are on the edge of wanting to do something, do it. The act of doing it is an accomplishment.

"There's a little bit of fear I have that time is running out. I have become much more conscious about time. We do not realise what we're exchanging time for. Time has become even more precious to me. I'm much more conscious about what time I'm giving away for each day that I exchange. Time is our most precious commodity. And yet for most of our lives, we treat it like we treat our good health; we take it for granted."

Carol

Time is uncontrollable. Therefore, it is essential to make each moment more precious than the last.

Instead of viewing it as an entity running out, view it as the time to start projects, whether professional or pleasure, rather than some catch-up period.

Let's use fifty as the marker of time. Post-fifty is your time to reinvent yourself (if you need to) and try out new things. Pre-fifty was the time dedicated to becoming you, even though you may not feel like you have changed that much over the years.

Becoming fifty-plus perfectly creates a frame to reinvent.

RISING REINVENTORS

The endless time we thought we had in the past can be an excuse not to get on with doing something. You can end up waiting for the next opportunity and the next. Over fifty, this concept disappears.

Life is more precious, which in itself is a positive. It's the perfect time to reset/start anything so that you can live without regret. We spend too much time stopping ourselves from doing anything – now, there is no time to waste.

"There's just no time to sit around saying to yourself, 'Oh, yeah, I'll do that another time."

Maryna

You have the luxury of knowing that time is no longer endless, which allows you to try and eliminate wasting time.

I hope by reading to this point you have now recognised that there's no such thing as wasting time, and everything happens as and when it's meant to.

You need to work your brain cells too. So, stay curious. To keep moving *Forward After Fifty* means no longer being stuck in the past, more like moving forward into the future.

Be curious

"You can't teach an old dog new tricks." We've all said it, heard it and used it often as an excuse not to try something. This well-known quote came from John Fitzherbert's *Book of Husbandry* (1523) and was literally for training dogs. The famous quote now refers to people who are unwilling to change their habits or who are stubborn.

Preparation/skill set

Don't underestimate the new tricks you can learn when you are willing to make an effort. If you have been led to believe that you have a worn-out ageing brain, then I'm sorry to inform you that's trash. It makes my hackles rise every time I hear a sixty-plus friend say, well, we are over sixty; therefore, it's a struggle to do this or that. Why? It's that crazy categorisation trap which we either fall or push others into, argh!!

For me, working to put a roof over my head and all the adult stuff meant learning new skills got side-tracked. I believe there's a period of your life where you use your practical learnings, which can become a little automated. Injecting new learnings can make you feel more fulfilled and help to kick-start your journey.

The post-fifty period allows new explorations. I believe women are better positioned to profit from these due to not being so dominated by our hormones. So yes, there are some advantages. Although learning about our bodies and how we function, to prevent health issues, is of utmost importance. Women have many opportunities to get in touch with their feminine energies despite menopause and negative connotations about ageing. We can stop pleasing other people and start pleasing ourselves.

Do you have your own business? You may not have considered this or dared to believe it possible for you. Yet you may find this statistic interesting from the USA – there are 114% more female entrepreneurs than 20 years ago. Although still only 4 out of 10 businesses are owned by women, the change is phenomenal.

RISING REINVENTORS

In 2020, UENI, a London-based tech company, undertook a survey of 22,257 businesses, and found that 7205 of these had been launched by female entrepreneurs. This represented 32% of the total, a massive uplift from a survey conducted four years previously when just 17% of founders were female. The future looks brighter, and we can be part of this growing movement. Forget the fountain of youth. Remember, you have a fountain of experience. The internet provides us with all the directions to the learning tools we need to start.

There is so much to learn when you run your own business. It's important to find out about crowdfunding, marketing, how other women have created their businesses, and so much more.

"I'm learning. And I have weeks where my brain is more in the past or worrying about the future more than it is focused on the present. So, it's an ongoing journey."

Karen

Good for the brain

Our education used the repetition tool, the 'learning hack' of today. So already, you're ahead of the game as you increase your skill set. Then, school was about having to learn. Now you choose to learn.

"No matter your age, your brain, like your muscles, grows through novelty so try something new each day."

Jim Kwik

I thought I would research brain exercises and came up with the following list:

- puzzles – jigsaws, crosswords, Sudoku
- play cards
- build your vocabulary
- dance
- use all your senses – touch, sight, smell, hearing and taste
- learn a new skill
- teach a skill
- listen to music.

Well, that seems relatively straightforward – time to be a little child-like and play.

I was not a good student until I left formal education to learn what I wanted to know. I've never considered myself academic, but as soon as I stopped caring what others thought I went 'back to school' and learnt how to:

- build two websites
- create a thriving networking group

- be a life coach
- create images for social media
- write blog posts
- do videos
- set up and host my podcast show
- use Instagram and so much more.

It's incredible what you can achieve when you let go of limiting beliefs and start believing that you are limitless. Try it and see what happens.

"Use your mind well. Keep curious and explore."

Kim

Everything is accessible

We live in a time where it couldn't be easier to learn absolutely anything. Whether building on what we already know (and we know a lot) or discovering new skills, we have no excuse. The internet is a powerful learning tool. If you want to learn basic instructions for a new skill, search for it on YouTube. That's what all ages do nowadays.

Adult learning is on offer in most places. There are many ways to train the brain. Luckily for us, it's very fashionable to do so. There are many courses and coaches, which is fantastic if you need to be persuaded that you can learn anything. A *Forward After Fifty* woman can learn something new at any age.

CHAPTER REFLECTION

- Your perception of time will make a difference to your life after fifty
- It's important to live in the now
- This is the time to start not stop
- Keep learning: it's good for your brain

TAKE ACTION

There is more than enough time to do all you want to do. Often lack of time is related to not prioritising and/or over-committing.

Time

Spend some time simplifying your life to create space for new things. A great place to start is with your diary:

- Go through your calendar/diary. Notice where you're overcommitting and/or attending unnecessary events.
- Delete entries where possible.
- Where not possible, consider their importance so that you can determine whether to commit to them going forward.

By making things simpler, you will be freeing up more time and energy for things you love doing, which leads us nicely into the task for curiosity.

Curiosity

Identify something that piques your curiosity and set aside some time to explore it further, i.e., *something in nature, a new hobby, travel etc.*

In the next chapter, we look into how to share your precious commodity, your wisdom, confidently.

Chapter 8

WISE NEW OWL

H ere we dive into acknowledging and sharing our wisdom.

I recently talked with a friend who was starting a master's degree at fifty. A professor on the interview panel asked her, "With all your experience, why not do a doctorate?"

Her initial reaction was, "Are you kidding?" Then she reminded herself that she had years of life/work experience under her belt, so it made sense. Five years later, she graduated and became a Doctor, feeling fabulously confident. She tapped into her wisdom. However, it took the professor to give her the nudge she needed to recognise that she had all the tools to go further.

My friend would describe herself as coming from a hard-working poor working-class background. She failed her 11-plus (a UK exam to assess entry-level students for selective secondary schools). But, despite that, she still went on to achieve great things. You don't have to be an academic, I'm certainly not. You can learn, as you go through your life so your school life/education doesn't need to define your outcome. It's your drive for change that counts.

Wisdom is not a measure of intelligence. What you have learned over the years is unique, an experience that is yours only. However, your knowledge and experience can benefit others. Don't hide it away.

"Wisdom is a new level of maturity and being able to feel good about things that you've achieved."

Maxine

Wisdom evolves throughout our timelines. Learnings from family, friends and acquaintances, good or bad, are taken and profited from.

Be your own person

To really enjoy and appreciate life after fifty, you need to become your own person, if you haven't already.

Janine shared that her biggest challenge has been integrating who she is rather than who she was. Her children have now left home, and through her personal experience and working with her clients, she has seen the gap that absence can leave in other people's lives. She started preparing herself ahead of time, leaving her wondering what her new role was. She questioned how she could turn her hobby into a business. You may have spent many years following other people's lead or looking after others, whereas now you can create newfound freedom. You need to permit yourself to do that first, though.

We all have an inner critic who can put us off doing the very things we desire to do.

For example, I like to write; however, I find writing quite tricky. This is often due to the voices from the past telling me that I'm not good enough on some level. So often, teachers' voices from childhood have little relevance to today, yet their messages are ingrained in our thinking.

You may find you perceive self-care as selfish, where you've been brought up to believe that you must put everyone else first.

You may also feel this way if self-care does not fit into your particular culture. While this cultural thinking doesn't fit in with how you want to be or what you want to do, you believe it is more important to follow the accepted culture than what you want or need.

Even spending money can be guilt-ridden if your parents were savers and disapproved of what they called 'wasting money', which perhaps was their belief system. Having nice things, having an expensive holiday, yes, having it all, can sometimes seem decadent. However, what if that holiday is fantastic and life-changing?

I had an aunt who was quite wealthy, and yet she darned her stockings until there were more darns than nylon. I hope she had pleasure from darning, and it was not because she had an inner critic telling her not to buy a new pair.

Seeking approval might have been the way you lived in the past. But it's time to change, as this thinking is holding you back. You are your own person and can create life on your terms. Will you look back on life and wish you'd followed everyone else's idea of how to live your life, or be grateful you chose to create your version of your best life?

It's time to reprogram the way you think. You do not need to ask permission from others anymore. You are an adult. A bit like reprogramming a computer, you can reframe your mindset and create an incredible life after fifty.

Many women I've interviewed for this book say being over fifty has been when they've gifted themselves the liberty to be free and make choices that suit them. Of course, some have interjected that it feels selfish, all of which can be echoes from parents/teachers.

Many women have had children, and their lives have been very much focused on their children's needs and wants. As the children leave the nest, a new sense of purpose needs to be created afresh.

Believe in yourself

"You're not wearing that!"

Carol mentioned that she remembers a time when she was going out with girlfriends for the night. She wore a pair of leather trousers she'd purchased after losing weight.

Feeling good and confident with her new body shape, she felt deflated when a friend said, "Well, who do you think you are wearing those?"

Were those judgmental remarks helpful? Anybody who heard that comment would likely start to think more negatively. However, there is a way to answer something like this when someone responds to you in this way.

What are the answers?

Instead of losing confidence, she could have come back with a response such as, "I'm a powerful woman ready to take on the world. Dressing like this helps me feel confident. You noticed me, so that's a good sign".

Sometimes you need to change your surroundings, not only the environment but the people you hang out with, to believe in yourself. People can be critical, but usually, it's more to do with what's going on with them than what's going on with you.

Don't let your inner critic take over and spiral you into thinking you're less worthy. We all do it, but it doesn't help you to move forward. It keeps you stuck.

Women can be their own worst enemies. Instead of focusing on our good internal qualities, we focus on external qualities around how we look, such as weight and wrinkles. Our looks seem to be more important than what we have to say.

What are limiting beliefs?

Limiting beliefs are simply beliefs that are limiting you in moving forward with your life. Those annoying voices in your head encouraging you to stay put.

"What is a belief? It's a feeling of certainty about what something means... Often, we are unconscious about what we believe and how those beliefs affect our actions. Our limiting beliefs can cause us to miss out on the things that we want most and our empowering beliefs can drive us toward to the life we want to live."

Tony Robbins

When we have limiting beliefs, we can end up over-thinking which can then lead to fears creeping in, trying to persuade us to stay where we are. If you think you have beliefs holding you back, book in a session with me to help you clear them. You do not need to hold onto them, no matter how long they have been hanging around.

In recognising which beliefs are holding you back, you can deal with them and move forward.

"I actually don't care anymore what people think."

Karen

"Don't let anything or anyone hold you back."

Maxine

"My biggest challenge has been to integrate who I actually am, rather than who I was."

Janine

Let go of judgement and overthinking

We are often judgemental without any knowledge of the personality or life of another person. We tend to judge people when it comes to their work, bodies, hair, and make-up, in fact, every little detail. We judge their homes, their choices, friends and family, animals and lives. With all this judgement, it's not surprising you can feel that you're judged in the same way, making change uncomfortable.

It's like going on stage in front of an audience of tear-you-apart critics. You may be wondering if someone will judge you. They are less likely to judge and more likely to care that you've done it in the first place. They might question if it is meaningful to them or not. The important thing is that you share your message, because it could make a difference, even if it's just to one person.

Since the '70s, magazines have influenced women to be self-conscious about their appearance and their relationships. It's all about attaining perfection and selling us the current commercial trends. But now we're beginning to see some magazines dealing with real-life issues that you and I might relate to. We are being treated like grown-up women, something that every woman deserves, no matter their age.

Many of the over-fifties women I've spoken to say, "I don't care what other people think anymore".

At long last, the liberty to be who you want to be. Being a certain age gives you the freedom to not worry about being judged by others. As a result, it can also mean you are less judgemental of others.

Give yourself permission to be you

We often seek permission without realising it. It can be that we are waiting until that permission is granted before we take action.

However, when you accept yourself, you no longer need permission. You grant it to yourself. Being less judgemental of others also helps you to be more compassionate towards yourself. Accept yourself for who you are right now. You do not need permission from anyone. Spend more time on yourself and less on others.

Part of my letting-go experience has been releasing people close to me; this sometimes means friends, even family. You can only genuinely be you if you surround yourself with people and environments where you feel free to be yourself.

It's time to permit yourself to be you – give it a go and see what happens. Let go a small step at a time.

"The question isn't who's going to let me; it's who's going to stop me."

Ayn Rand

Bad experiences/mistakes

How useful are they? I've concluded that they deserve more credit. Why's that, you may wonder?

A broken relationship, a job loss, personal losses, bad health, financial loss, are all challenges that feel deeply disturbing, which can make you feel physically sick and disempowered.

I've encountered all these emotions, yet I choose to take these experiences as essentials to my life. They've made me feel stronger and more authentic than ever before and have equipped me to move forward. Here are some of my examples.

I was in a relationship that possessed me for five years. It was complicated and exciting at the same time. However, I suffered mentally and then practically as I lent money to the person in question who went off with someone else – an affair with plenty of cliches. Thinking back, I made a lucky escape. Heart hormones were dominating me, which can be dangerous.

I love the saying 'rejection is protection' because I wasted so much emotion on feeling sorry for myself when I could have been jumping for joy at my getaway. My mistake of lending money to this character taught me not to do that again too.

My next mistake was to waste time on reflecting why had I lost a job at 56. I humiliated myself by trying to crawl back to the job and bought into the ageist view that finding another one would be challenging. Later, I started to embrace the change which allowed me to leap forward into something new. This last experience was the turning point of realising that these mistakes and bad experiences were life-savers.

When I have experiences now that are not so happy, I turn the lessons gained from the past into positives. For example, an involvement for eight years in an over-eighty-year-old man's fight against two people who took his savings has seemed like living a soap opera. It has been difficult and dark at times.

Instead of wallowing, I have chosen to look upon this experience constructively. Perhaps my turning this experience into a book or a soap opera and making it public might help people who find themselves in the same situation.

Turning negative experiences into positive lessons is good for your health and reinvention. You can choose to stay stuck or let go and move into your future self.

"So, when I find that it's not perfect, and compare against what I used to do, or be, then sometimes I may feel like a failure. I've recently been reframing my mindset and thinking less about expectations, but about the goals that I want to achieve. It's all about progress and not perfection."

Lisa

CHAPTER REFLECTION

- Wisdom is underrated. Give yourself the credit you deserve
- Wisdom is not a measure of intelligence but what you have learned over the years
- Be inspirational to others, share your wisdom
- Remember, all your experiences have been essential in creating the unique person that you are now.

TAKE ACTION

Are you tapping into your wisdom or discounting all your experience?

To tap into your wisdom:

- Write a brief timeline of your key experiences in life, and the lessons you've learned from them.
- Consider ways that you can share your learnings with others.
- Remember, your wisdom can make a massive difference to one person.

In the next chapter, we're going to be uncovering one of the biggest fears that comes up as people age – the fear of losing your independence. I'll be sharing how this doesn't have to be the end of the road, and ways you can stay independent as you move *Forward After Fifty*.

Chapter 9

INDEPENDENT WOMAN

Concern regarding independence was an issue mentioned frequently by my interviewees. Superpowered women want independence. The fear of not being independent is very real on your journey *Forward After Fifty*. We expect age to take our independence away, whether physically, mentally or financially.

So often, a cultural attitude means that we believe it is inevitable; however, times have changed since our parents' generation.

You have choices; you can sit back and wait for age to get you or you can do something about it.

Almost everything in this book will help you be independent if you actively do something about it. The first steps are to stop reading and speaking about age negatively.

Take note of the longevity recipe: stay social, exercise mind and body, eat with care, sleep wisely; all of this is free and in your hands.

Choosing the right environment

The women before me, namely my mother and grandmother, had complete independence until the age of eighty-eight. They made their own decisions, lived in their own homes and lived the life they'd always been living. All this changed due to suffering from falls, as many women unfortunately experience as they age.

As mentioned previously, in some countries, there aid available to create home comfort. Simple adjustments such as ramps and bars could make the difference to staying in your environment, which surely most people desire.

The problem is that none of us tends to think about this until it's too late.

Cost and age-denial figures in this too.

My grandmother lived until ninety-six, in a nursing home for the last eight years of her life. She was very sociable, and I think being with others suited her – retirement living/senior living housing, which is more available today, would have been her perfect solution.

My mother lives in her own, yet again, impractical home.

Independent living is a huge concern; like exercise, physical and mental preparation for ageing is of utmost importance, so are other practicalities. If I base my own life on the women before me, I could easily have thirty more years ahead. Do you agree preemption is better than cure? Being prepared is essential.

Choosing your environment, whatever it may be – within your own four walls, assisted living, intergenerational living, living near family – is a step in the right independence direction.

The importance of connection

In my experience of female networking, group connection has been tested and is paramount. Unfortunately, despite the miracle of Zoom and FaceTime communication, it became apparent in the pandemic that there is no substitute for close contact with other people.

Environment, culture and circumstances impact communities, sometimes bringing unwelcome loneliness. Disconnection can lead to depression and fear, which crushes your confidence, which is hardly conducive to having and using your superpowers. Connection makes us feel worthwhile, allows us to learn from each other, create together, exchange emotions, laugh and cry. We are social, not solitary animals.

While living in Italy during the seventies, I remember being impressed and curious by people gathering in the fountain-focused squares. I watched as people held a gelato (ice-cream) in one hand whilst the other hand gesticulated in expressive conversation. Evening walks were a joyous chance to enjoy the favourable weather and connect with fellow humanity.

Even confined in apartment block living which I experienced in Italy, it made little difference. One still went outside to eat ice cream. Sunny places make a splendid excuse to connect.

However, cold countries such as Finland, which has the highest ageing population after Japan, try to keep a connected ageing society due to the ageing explosion. There is heavy investment in keeping people in their own homes. For example, funding is in place to provide for mobility issues, such as ramps and walking aids. Institutionalised homes for the elderly are often directed only towards the very needy. The goal is to keep everyone in their own homes. The high target rate of 92% of the ageing population to remain in their own homes is impressive - all this is outlined in *Finland's Ageing Policy*.

As a result, information centres for Finland's ageing population are already in place where you can update your skills, exercise and socialise. Access is at the top of the list – access to towns and access inside your home. So, a cold climate is no excuse to be isolated.

When I was in my early twenties, I lived in different countries, which was more an adventure than a permanent decision. That came at forty-something when Alain and I moved from the city to a small village in France. Over the years, my connections, due to travelling away from home a great deal, seemed relatively paltry.

Instead, I noticed a reliance on my mother's friendship, who lives close by.

I knew I had to make other connections so that my life didn't become too insular. Not having enough social interactions can inspire you to explore places to connect; the alternative is to be alone. Language barriers can become like walls, too, so we seek people of our native language. Fortunately, in my case, English is spoken by so many people and I feel very grateful for this.

Building on my idea of connecting with more people, I created a networking group in Provence to establish business opportunities and friendships and explore how being connected works. Of course, there's effort involved in taking on such a sizeable project, which can be uncomfortable but necessary. However, the return on that effort has been enormous.

We live in a world of strange parallels, the connected and disconnected.

The television, for example, has replaced family and friends around the fire conversation. Intrusively placed in the centre of our homes, a tool that can talk at us but not with us.

We find ourselves in a world where social media keeps us connected; we need to use this to our advantage. It took me a while to join Facebook and other social media platforms. The sound of superficial relationships didn't appeal, and in 2011 I didn't understand how it functioned. Now, though, I have come to realise that:

Social media has kept me connected with many people I wouldn't or couldn't physically meet otherwise.

Being online expands your world. Social media is a part of our lives now, so to keep up to date, you need to move with the times. It is an excellent way to share information, create virtual friendships and expand connections far and wide. These incredible online social platforms can help us remain connected.

My friend Karen, widowed, took her future into her own hands, moved back to her own country into a new-build home within a small development. Everyone is in the same boat, equal whatever age, race or sexual preference. So, even though all alone in their new homes in a new place, they created a community together.

People eat and drink together, protect and beautify the external gardens, and hold events – a real sense of community. Karen has never looked back. This is an example of how community can work. A common theme can start a community of like-minded people from different backgrounds, a connection based on a sense of purpose.

Connecting allows you to share your skills; there's now an opportunity like never before through the internet. You can connect your vision, business, project, and ideas to the world.

Albeit a pandemic, Covid has taught us that connections are of utmost importance for everybody's wellbeing, whatever age group you find yourself in. It taught us that being with people from different age groups, and outside our usual circles, is preferable to living in isolation.

Scotland is one country that is aiming to be intergenerational by 2030. Generations Working Together is an organisation in Scotland (generationsworkingtogether.org) dedicated to making this happen. This means cultivating connection on a grand scale, where no categorisation occurs, young or old. A melting pot of talents that can produce self-esteem, exchange of knowledge, the passing of wisdom, and a forward-thinking society of true equality is exciting news!

"Create ways to get out and interact with people, even if it's just online."

Janine

Make technology a priority

If you haven't already done so, prepare for your independence. Let's change the expectation that you will be dependent on others in your later years. People in their eighties/nineties are now a generation who have found themselves older than they may have anticipated, and the world has not prepared the best solutions for this change.

We are now seeing what works and what doesn't, so we are in an excellent position to eliminate what we don't want to happen.

Moreover, there's often money to be made behind this concept: medication, retirement homes to name a few.

Financial support is of utmost importance. Take the time to learn how to do online banking or banking through an app. It will give you independence and control. It will allow you to get your finances in order.

One of my friends, who is in her seventies, has rented homes in several countries to feed her desire to travel. She is now exploring ways to live in a cooperative, solely designed with the fifties and upwards in mind, or intergenerational. Whatever age you are, you can enhance your life with physical or mental support. My friend believes a cooperative would give her the support she needs as she enters the next phase of her life.

In an ideal world, we would have more workplaces supporting independence rather than taking it away as our dates of birth go further back.

Investing in your physical and mental health can help create independence. In addition, you can prevent issues that might arise by taking control through good nutrition, exercise, brain exercise – everything discussed in this book.

Make the decision today to always stay independent. Rather than relying on others, rely on yourself from now on. Create a plan *now* always to stay independent.

Age vulnerability

The word vulnerability has come up repeatedly in my interviewee conversations. There can be many reasons for feeling more vulnerable as we get older. Poor health is one of the top reasons. For example, when you are unwell, you can be at the mercy of others and lose some of your independence. I hope that future generations will attend to age vulnerability more aggressively.

With an ageing population and how our lives have evolved, sometimes elderly relatives end their lives in a care home. However, there are positive signs that this form of segregation will end with intergeneration unless in exceptional circumstances. A 20th-century solution is no longer necessary in a non-ageist 21st century.

I have witnessed on more than one occasion how our ageist world can treat those in care. So, unfortunately, the word 'care' would not even be a word I would use regarding how some elderly can be so poorly treated.

Sadly, I have had first-hand experience of poor treatment, both with my mother and my husband's father. Doctors would medicate the elderly with sleeping tablets, and television was used regularly as a pacifier in my father-in-law's home. We do not become less of a human as we age. Instead, we might well need more love and kindness.

Another sad story was of an 80-something-year-old desperate to sell his cold and basic house with facilities that did not match his needs. In desperation to sell, he was robbed, not by a monster with fangs and green skin, but by seemingly ordinary people who saw an opportunity. His vulnerability led him to trust strangers who convinced him that they could invest his money so that he would become wealthier. Being alone, having financial issues, and having mental health concerns can contribute to vulnerability. It's important to know who you can trust.

Without a doubt, societies need to make radical changes. I don't have the answers, but I believe we can help our destiny with an empowered attitude.

I recently read a report by Age UK. They were responding to the vulnerability around banking and the lack of straightforward and secure facilities for the elderly. In addition, technology is speeding up, which can leave the elderly bewildered. Some do not know how to access online banking or navigate the process.

While some of us embrace technology, others find the jargon challenging. For example, I remember a conversation concerning a banking app not functioning as I expected. As a result, I contacted my bank and was treated dismissively, as if I was a cyber moron.

Be more determined now that you're over fifty. It's time to become savvy. Keep up with technology, connect on and offline, be financially strong.

Could the answer be to have a better age range of people serving? There needs to be a greater focus on intergenerational employees and employment for pensioners with training. Perhaps this would lead to less exclusion. And a better understanding amongst different age groups.

Carers too need more support. There's a strong likelihood that you will become a carer within the family. Statistics suggest that you may dedicate seventeen years of your life to looking after an elderly parent. This would not necessarily need to be an issue if we took the 'prevention vs cure' approach, where we take responsibility for our wellbeing or like in Finland create accessible housing as an alternative to living away from other age groups in residential homes for the elderly.

In an ideal world, this will all be made more accessible through the development of an anti-ageist culture and society, but there is generally still a long way to go.

A friend of mine chose to live with her elderly parents, leaving her family, husband and adult children. She told me she found herself being a stranger in her own home and with her parents too. With one parent with Alzheimer's and another with cancer, she experienced just how complex the world of caring is.

In the UK, financial support is not abundant. My friend had to discover how it worked, what help she could get, and like so many after a couple of years, she no longer had the facilities at their home to look after their needs. The property had to be sold to finance expensive care.

Creating financial independence

Being truly independent often comes with managing your money well. When you are a good money manager, you're not as dependent on others supporting you in different areas of your life.

> *When you're in control of your money, you have more choice.*

Conversely, when you aren't in control of your finances, you're reliant on others, potentially putting yourself in victim mode and needing to be rescued. You get to choose to be independent.

To become more independent, you need to look at the stories you're telling yourself about your money story.

How well do you manage your finances? You may be a great money manager, and if that's the case, you can skip this section. However, if money makes you want to retreat, you're allowing money to control you, which places you in victim mode. Read on.

My money story is of a person who doesn't look at their accounts. My partner is a very good money manager. Because of that, my interest in money has grown. I learnt that I had a money story that needed to be transformed. Often our money stories stem from childhood. I had one parent who held onto money and another who let it all go.

Conversely, let me tell you about one of my friends. Maxine's financial independence was the most significant and crucial factor in her sixties and throughout her adult life. She generated her income, and with that, she said it gave her the freedom to do whatever she wished, whether investing in a business, self-development or travelling with friends. She had been married for 40 years and financially she and her husband were equal because she had independence in her relationship.

So, if you have practised independence throughout your life, it's time to celebrate. If not, this is the perfect time to start.

Being independent can also mean letting go of what others are thinking and concentrating on being your own best friend. It can mean listening to yourself and trusting your judgement. Don't overthink. Let go and do your own thing.

I guess the question arises of can we be accessible within a relationship, whether the family or a partnership? When you're in a family environment or sharing a home with someone, there can be an element of compromise with decision-making. Making decisions for others and delegating can be easier than making the same for oneself.

Blossoming alone for some echoes selfishness, but how can you be accused of being selfish when you are simply looking after your own needs? Dedicating our lives to others to then find that we are left alone can be difficult. No matter what relationship you're in, being independent on some level can be empowering.

RISING REINVENTORS

When I was nineteen, I worked for an American family in Italy. The children's upbringing was very different to mine, the girls seemed so independent. Their mother said she wanted her girls to be independent so that if something happened to her, they could carry on as if nothing had happened. I was full of admiration for this ethos. And as my friend Maxine says, "In the end, we have to look out for ourselves to achieve certain things. You cannot look to someone else to help achieve that".

Cultural differences

Depending on culture, money may be a tricky subject. For example, in America, many people love to talk about money. However, the Brits tend to feel uncomfortable when the money subject arises.

Do you plan to live in a retirement home? Start putting aside some money as they can be a considerable investment if you do. Unfortunately, misfortune often falls on families, resulting in having to sell the family home to fund a place for their elderly parent(s). It would be so much better if the goal was to keep people in their own homes.

I truly hope retirement will become a thing of the past. I would encourage you to forget about the word altogether and embrace your age.

Let's be like what they are doing in Finland, as mentioned earlier. Let's invest in ourselves now by being independent.

In 2020, Belgium, France, Denmark, Latvia, Luxembourg, Sweden, Canada, Iceland, Portugal and Ireland were the only countries in the world offering full equal rights for men and women, according to Statista (statista.com).

Sadly, this and the over-fifties education system have created a likelihood that you may not be managing your finances correctly or even looking at them. If money management were taught in schools, it would make such a difference to the economy.

*Independence doesn't mean being alone.
However, it does mean taking control of
your destiny and not relying on others.*

What's your money story like?

Ask yourself the following questions to find your level of independence. There is often a lot of fear around money. Check in with yourself:

- Do you have your own bank account?
- How often do you look at it?
- Do you know how to run your home finances?
- Do you hang out with people you want to be with regularly, without your partner being present?
- Are you physically and mentally travelling to places you want to go to?
- Are you investing in yourself or others?
- Are you living how you want to live – in the best of circumstances?

If you're worried about looking at your bank account, remember this: it doesn't matter how much or little you have there. Just checking is raising your awareness of your money situation.

"I wanted to be an independent woman, a woman who could pay for her bills, a woman who could run her own life – and I became that woman."

Diane von Furstenberg

Once you know the balance, you can determine whether you are in control of your finances or not. That knowledge can empower you to create a better money story from now on.

RISING REINVENTORS

If you are reading this, you are likely to have been educated in the sixties/seventies/eighties. The 1960s were a transformational time for women in many senses. More women than ever started to work, and the pill gave women a choice to have children or not. Yet women's education at that time was still attached to the idea of creating second-class citizens, women who didn't ask for much.

Lessons were gender-dominated. Cooking was for girls, and technical drawing was for boys. Even girls wearing trousers at school was revolutionary. We were moulded into women who would have to expect to be dependent.

Most of us are not living in extended families, and many of us who have had elderly grandparents and parents have experience of the need to use care homes.

Research says that a 50-year-old has a 53% to 59% chance of entering a care home of some sort in their lifetime. So, it's no wonder that my interviewees universally mentioned they were concerned about independence or the lack of it.

That's why it is so important to protecting your independence by remaining healthy in mind and body where possible and, importantly, being able to use online tools. You might feel overwhelmed but keeping up with the modern world is the key to your independence.

The computerised world at a touch will inform and connect you, so accept it. Try to include it in your day-to-day exploration.

CHAPTER REFLECTION

Since our mother's generation, we've come on in leaps and bounds to become independent women.

- Take control of your money to give yourself more options.
- Make the decision **today** to always stay as independent as possible. Feel empowered. Rely on yourself rather than relying on others. Conversely, if ill health does prevail, it shows great courage to ask for the help you need.
- Keep up with technology, connect on and offline, be financially strong, and exercise!

TAKE ACTION

- Write a list of ways you can create more independence in your life.
- Next to each item on the list write down a solution and a plan of action.

Let's take that further by taking the practical action to be fearless instead of fearful about losing your independence – *Forward After Fifty*.

In the next chapter, we embrace the more spiritual side of our superpowers, exploring gratitude and forgiveness.

Chapter 10

THE POWER OF GRATITUDE AND FORGIVENESS

Throughout this book we've talked about how you can age positively.

Gratitude is a wonderful way to celebrate everything that is happening in your life now and up to this point.

Thinking positively about ageing can be a challenge. After all, most of us have been educated to expect the worst, but somehow, you can funnel all your doubts into hopes with gratitude.

Negative emotions can be powerful too. They help us understand ourselves and what is going on and appreciate all the good emotions that come too. Without one, you don't experience the other in the same way.

A friend summed up gratitude perfectly – "It's free medicine".

The value of gratitude

So, let's see how gratitude works:

Humans are naturally drawn to the 'negative bias' described by psychologists, where we not only notice negativity but dwell on it. In addition, bad news and experiences trigger something in our brains; this is often known as our protective instinct.

We like to laugh, not cry; love, be happy, not sad. However, some negative emotions seem uncontrollable, even non-negotiable. Sometimes we can even feel guilty for not feeling sad.

However, shifting into a place of gratitude gives a calmer feeling. Dwelling on the positive instead of the negative helps you deal with life's challenges – an aid to looking after oneself, which puts you in a better place to look after others.

Sit down and think of one thing you are grateful for. Write it down. You can choose something big or small. Once you have it written down, you may want to add another. This simple routine can shift into your superpower.

My best friend has had numerous operations ever since she was very young. Unlike many of us who will question, "Why me?", instead, she says, "Why not me?" She is always grateful for the times she has good health.

We all experience good and bad times, and daily gratitude is scientifically proven to support us. It doesn't come in the form of a pill; it's not a quick fix, but the immediate difference is a free and easily doable daily practice.

Create a gratitude practice yourself – you can do it in the morning or the evening. Gratitude in the evening can give you pleasant thoughts to help you drift off to sleep, and morning gratitude can help set up your day. It's all about focusing on appreciating things you might have taken for granted.

Gratitude increases our confidence; it empowers and helps us appreciate what others do. So, simple salutations such as a smile or a knowing nod are heartfelt and promote positivity.

Gratitude can help anger management. My father had a lot to be desired as a role-model father; however, I am grateful for certain aspects of his personality. Thanks to him, I was born. If you are thankful for the positives, it's easier to deal with the negatives.

What can you be grateful for today?

Ask yourself that simple question: "What can I be grateful for today?" A moment in nature, a smile, a kind word, a gift, a phone call?

Gratitude can transform common days into thanksgiving, turn routine jobs into joy, and change ordinary opportunities into blessings.

Proverb

Practising gratitude

In a *Thrive Global* interview, Tony Robbins proves that this free medication takes no time at all. He shared:

"I do three things for 3 1/3 minutes each: I focus on three moments in my life that I'm grateful for because gratitude is the antidote to the things that mess us up.

You can't be angry and grateful simultaneously. You can't be fearful and grateful simultaneously. So, gratitude is the solution to both anger and fear. So, instead of just acting grateful, I think of specific situations that I'm thankful for, little ones and big ones. I do it every day, and I step into those moments and feel gratitude and aliveness."

Turn frustration into gratitude

Imagine you're waiting for a vital parcel you've stayed in to receive; however, the postman arrives without it. Frustration arises, turning into anger, all not good for one's health.

Could you stop for a moment and be grateful that someone comes with the post at all, how it's been transported, and all the people involved to make that happen? How does that make you feel? It's a simple example of how gratitude practice could help make your life easier.

Maybe you are experiencing regret about not having achieved some goals or that marriage that went wrong. Now you're over fifty, facing a different life can bring exasperation at all the things you wish had gone better.

Gratitude for the experiences of a soured marriage or even the children it brought into your life might help you move forward and out of a dark place. When you're a child of such a union like myself, an example of positivity like this in difficult times can make a meaningful difference.

Be grateful for age; many have never experienced or will experience this part of life. It's full of superpower opportunities. One opportunity is that ageing doesn't have to be miserable, unhealthy or a process of decline. We have so many inexpensive tools to make it one of the most pleasurable times of your life, including gratitude.

"Enjoy the little things, for one day you may look back and realize they were the big things."

Robert Brault

POSITIVE THOUGHTS 50+

If you are still at this point thinking that you're not grateful for anything, that your life is a nightmare where everything goes wrong, then I'd like you to pause for a moment. Think of three things in your life that are going well, and express gratitude for them.

There are times when it can feel wrong to practise gratitude. For example, it might feel distasteful for you to feel gratitude when you know so many people are suffering, making you feel guilty. So, let me pose this question to you – is not being thankful for your life going to help them? If you want to help, create a plan and make it happen!

RISING REINVENTORS

It's normal to align ourselves with the situation when friends or family find themselves miserable or fabulous. My mother, 91 at the time of writing, has mobility issues. Her life is a lot more constricted than it was several years ago.

Relations and friends will say, "Oh no, poor Betty". Yet, I say it's fantastic she's still here. She can choose to adapt to her circumstances and still have a fulfilled life. It just means that she has to explore this in a different way i.e., via a computer. Life is short; the longer you live, the more there is to explore.

Personal development often comes when your journey changes. Fifty-five, my normality shattered. The routine mammogram results didn't work out; I was so confident of my good health I believed a mistake must have occurred.

Several months later, I, along with others, was culled from my job at a company to which I'd dedicated many working years. I felt trapped and undeserving of all this disappointment. I didn't see that this was the release from a life that no longer served me.

Unknowingly I had a lot to be grateful for, and I could have stopped wasting valuable time feeling humiliated. Instead, I could have used gratitude to empower myself. Looking back now, I recognise I was fortunate that this sequence of events led me to explore life coaching, which brought the tool of gratitude practice.

Here are some questions to ponder:

- Is it more empowering to be happy or sad?
- Is it wiser to feel content with your current circumstances and ready to create more of what you love?
- What will be helpful for you and the people around you?

Gratitude puts you in a happier state of mind, as despite everything going on around you, you can still choose to focus on things to be grateful for. I believe it's healthier to be positive. What about you?

Exercising forgiveness

If I think of forgiveness, I think of it being something that I need to do to let other people off the hook. However, if you know the Buddhist beliefs around this, you'll understand that it's about releasing yourself from something painful that someone has 'done to you'. While forgiveness is part of our culture, it can be a challenge.

When you feel angry about something that has happened to you or any other negative emotion, the emotion affects you and not the other person. When you practise forgiveness, you release that connection between you and the other person. You choose to let go of the negative emotion surrounding that experience, allowing you to move on.

Forgiveness can give you a sense of freedom to take the next step, to shift in a different direction.

Regret raised its head in my interviewee conversations, for example, staying in an unsatisfactory relationship or job. But, over fifty, you can choose to ponder on the past or let it go and create a more fun and progressive life.

Instead of blaming others or yourself, forgive yourself instead. See what worked, not what didn't. A lousy marriage may have given life to others; I think of myself as a daughter of one of those bad marriages. If my parents hadn't split up, my half-siblings, nieces and nephews wouldn't have been born.

Forgiving others who have made your life hell could give you release. Simple, but not easy. Parts of my childhood were unenviable; an alcoholic parent, their aggression and everything that goes with it. However, I decided to practise forgiveness in my adult life and look upon my father as a friend with issues rather than the responsible, perfect father we all wish we had; it helped. Still twinges of rage bubble forth, during parent discussions with my siblings, and we're all over forty, meaning these emotions can last forever. It helps to recognise, label and move the emotions aside to get on with your one only precious life.

Choosing happiness

Choosing happiness can sometimes bring all kinds of issues to the surface. You *can* choose happiness. It's time to recognise you deserve to be happy, and equally be OK when you're sad.

Sometimes we spend so much time thinking of the happiness of others that we forget ourselves, and we believe that everyone else has forgotten us too. Then we feel lonely and unhappy; investing in yourself and your happiness is crucial.

Bhutan, a kingdom in the Himalayas, South Asia, focuses on happiness, so much so they measure happiness and wellbeing using a Happiness Index.

As a tour director, years ago, I was fortunate enough to have some members of the Bhutanese royal family join me on tour. They made me aware of the GDP of Happiness, something I had never heard of before.

In my research, I learned that happiness is considered a 'fundamental human goal' there, and when changes are introduced, it is with a strong focus on improving citizens' wellbeing.

Everybody has good and bad experiences in life. If we had constant happiness, we perhaps wouldn't appreciate the beauty in life, as we wouldn't have the contrast of the darker times. Balance is inescapable and a necessary part of life; we need lows to have highs.

If you haven't started practising gratitude yet, it can allow you to appreciate the big and small delights of life. You can find happiness in the small moments.

Dr Julie Smith, a well-known clinical psychologist, writes, "Happiness is a by-product of living in line with our values, and we feel it in balance with all the other human emotions".

According to research, the older we are, the happier we become. An interesting analysis if you read all that ageing negativity throughout the years. I don't ever remember feeling excited about ageing. Instead, I didn't even want to think about it.

Happiness, when you're over fifty, is different. Self-analysis and experience make you aware of what you want in your life. All that's been before brings you to a different perspective, which often makes you want to make significant changes.

Pressures of the past, such as being rich and famous and recognised for who you are, may no longer figure in your life.

You may no longer be waiting for others to make you happy.

Happiness does come with a positive mindset; however, accepting that it's also OK to sit with your feelings is essential. It is OK to be sad, fed up, and all the other emotions. They are part of the balance of life. Balance is the key; you don't have to be happy all the time, and you can be sad. The beauty of ageing is that you can, at last, be yourself.

Decisions that were perceived wrong at the time often become regrets. Instead, think of them as pointers in the right direction, adding to a significant tool bag full of experiences that will guide you forward. For example, our superpower, experience, brings us closer to contentment. You know what you don't and do like; living your core values means living your life authentically. You'll be in the position to understand why something makes you feel as you do, and that peace of mind creates a state of happiness.

My great friend David died in 2006, not long after my fiftieth birthday, from Aids. I regret dearly not having persuaded him to take the Aids test he'd always resisted; it might have saved his life. I regret wasting time doing insignificant jobs; I regret not telling a few people what I thought of their behaviour. I regret staying in a tired-out relationship. I regret being held back by my limiting beliefs.

All of us have had situations where deep regret is involved, but we can only do what we can with the skills, tools and experience at our disposal at that time. We can only move on, whatever the regret. However, we can use these situations to gain insights that we can now use in this period of our lives.

Past events that you might label as regrets may have led you down a different path. Yet, whatever decisions you have made will have armed you with wisdom.

Here are my 3 top tips to creating happiness:

1. If a smile from someone creates happiness, smile first.
2. If genuine happiness for other people's success makes you happy, surround yourself with uplifting people.
3. Create a happy environment, be with people you want to be with, in a place you want to live/stay.

CHAPTER REFLECTION

Gratitude is appreciating the little day-to-day experiences you might have taken for granted: birdsong, the different colours of the leaves, an acknowledgement from a passer-by. It increases our confidence and is a great inspiration to start this practice.

- Be grateful for your age; many have never experienced or will experience this part of life. I suspect that we all know someone who has passed and not experienced being over fifty, sixty and onwards. I do, and I know that those people would have done anything to swap their circumstances for ours.
- Forgiveness is key to living a happier life. Let go of the need to hold onto anger and resentment. Remember, you're not letting the other person off the hook by forgiving them, you're freeing yourself.
- Waiting for happiness can be a long investment; creating it can start today as you move *Forward After Fifty*.

TAKE ACTION

Gratitude is an empowering formula to allow you to stay mindful, no matter what is going on around you. It has the power to uplift you mentally, emotionally, physically and spiritually.

Gratitude

Create a mini daily gratitude practice:

- **Morning:** Identify 3 things you're currently grateful for
- **Evening:** Identify the best thing that happened that day

Forgiveness can be a way to release resentments and empower yourself. Holding onto resentment can create bad energy. Letting go can be liberating.

Forgiveness

Consider a situation that is making you feel resentful. Are you about to give up on someone or something? Check in with yourself first. How would applying forgiveness to this situation help you?

In the next chapter, we're talking about how it's possible to create the happiness you deserve as you move *Forward After Fifty*.

Chapter 11

YOUR FUTURE SELF

I love the analysis of the miracle of simply being here. In a TEDx talk, Mel Robbins, a riotously funny self-help author, mentioned that scientists estimate the probability of you being born is at about one in 400 trillion.

Yes, the probability of your parents meeting etc. Mine met in the theatre where they both were working and then married after six weeks of knowing each other, and then I came along, so I can relate to being a miracle. You are too.

You are a miracle with an assigned time on the planet, and therefore you deserve the best. You can make a difference for yourself and others. You might be more aware of that now that you are nearing or are over fifty. Now is the perfect time to create a future life plan.

RISING REINVENTORS

When you are a twenty-year-old, the grown-ups will be asking all kinds of questions about your future. A fifty-year-old will better know their wants without grown-ups pressurising them. Equipped with experiences, you know what you don't want and don't like. Therefore, you can choose to start/continue your quest for a fulfilled life after fifty.

Fifty and over can present life challenges that can impact your life in many ways, such as your career, losing partners through relationship changes or grief, or your children becoming adults and leaving home.

As we age, there can be times when we feel challenged emotionally. We can feel fragile, humiliated, sad, depressed, hopeless, empty, frightened, and pessimistic. Yet, these are times when we can learn how to build our resilience, choose to rise, and make positive changes in our lives.

Many opportunities are not obvious, disguised by sudden and often unwelcome changes. Still, these are moments when life can go in a completely different direction. Disempowerment can turn into empowerment. You are in the driving seat; what address will you put in the GPS?

I know of two people who have suffered bereavement in the last couple of years; one remains in the past, posting pictures on social media of good times gone. She sits in front of the TV and lives a sedentary life.

The other started a new life by moving countries, where she made new friends in a newly-built community. She now runs various events to draw the community together. Imagining loss brings deep emotional feelings, yet if you look at the story of these two, who would you prefer to be?

"I don't need to look back, I can just keep looking to the future saying, 'Right, I'd like to do this and try that'".

Maxine

I lost a job that I'd become accustomed to, which meant my immediate future self didn't expect change. Although it took some time, I understood that time was precious when I lost this job.

> **Unexpected life events can allow you to make changes and create different experiences for yourself.**

Once over the initial ageist limiting belief that being over fifty would mean that nobody would want to employ me, I knew I only had myself to answer to. I could rise to the challenge or give in to it and accept my fate.

We've all been through a period of loss during the 2020/21 pandemic, in varying degrees. For some, they have lost their freedom, jobs and even loved ones. Some have waited for their previous careers to restart, and others have taken the opportunity to change. Ruth Ribeaucourt, who had been creating successful retreats, told me that sitting at her kitchen table, she wondered what the hell she was going to do. She considered selling her collection of accumulated buys of antique market items. However, she put everything into a dream of creating a printed magazine, *Faire*, for creatives. When the regular printers were going out of business, she set up a new business, which has since become a worldwide success.

CHAPTER REFLECTION

Any change you put in place now will impact your future self.

- You are a miracle. The chances of you being here at this time are 1 in 400 trillion.
- Trying times can be a turning point of opportunity.
- You have the tools to take control of your future self as you move *Forward After Fifty*.

TAKE ACTION

Trying times can be a turning point of opportunity – where your choice can help you create a better future self. On that note, Natalie MacNeil, an entrepreneur, inspired me to write a letter to my future self, a process she shares in her ritual book.

It's a powerful process where you explore how you want your future self to be. You consider areas such as financial comfort, a free lifestyle, confidence, happiness, new connections, a new business and relaxation. All things that you might not have stopped to consider in full before. Once you've written the letter, you put it away for a long period of time and review it later. If elements of your letter feel out of reach, create a plan to move forward.

- Spend some time writing a letter to your future self. What do you wish for her in the future?
- Once you've written your letter, create a plan of action to make it happen.

In the next chapter, we'll do a recap of the journey you've taken throughout this book, and I'll share with you how you can move *Forward After Fifty* with my help.

Chapter 12

SUMMARY & WHAT'S NEXT

I hope this book has encouraged or inspired you positively to start or even consider reinvention as you move *Forward After Fifty*.

We've been on a journey together. It started when we talked about ageism and how, together, we can begin to eliminate this unjust prejudice, starting with our own behaviour.

We then talked about the importance of understanding yourself through learning and living in alignment with your values – your priceless superpower tool.

We discussed the all-important area of mindset, where I shared some things you can do to strengthen your mindset so that you start to view ageing differently. Next, we explored how wellbeing is in your hands despite the media and others telling you that you're on your way out. You can take many preventative measures to prolong your life and enhance its quality.

We then explored what a career reboot might be like, including ideas to make it fun, profitable and doable. And then we talked about how time is precious and how you have so much more time than you perhaps thought. We talked about how curiosity is vital to use to keep up in our modern world.

Having talked about time and curiosity, we then reflected on your unique superpower – wisdom.

In Chapter 9, you learned some of what it takes to be an independent woman. Then, in the last two chapters, we looked at gratitude and how being grateful can shift your mindset. And finally, we explored that it's possible to choose happiness over regret and sadness, to go forward after fifty.

What's next?

Your journey does not have to stop here. If you have enjoyed this book, you'll love my 30-day email series, *30 Days to Kick-start Your Life After 50*, where you get daily email inspiration and prompts to start your reinvention journey.

If you'd prefer to work 1:1, then book a Reinvention Planning Session with me where we will work together for 2 hours to create your bespoke reinvention plan. No more feeling lost, lacking confidence, or feeling that age is limiting you. Instead, step into your power, be fearless and live your best life after fifty.

Now you can choose more resilience to live Forward After Fifty, fully, fabulously and with an empowered attitude.

Here's to being and supporting Superpowered Rising Reinventors!

You can download my free workbooks,

- *The Secret to Ageing Positively:* rebeccaronane.com/the-secret-to-ageing-positively/,
- *Forward After Fifty Workbook:* rebeccaronane.com/faf-50-workbook/.

See my Reinvention program

- *30 Days to Kick-start Your Life After 50:* rebeccaronane.com/30-days-to-kick-start-your-life-after-50/

Until we meet again, here's to your reinvention!

Rebecca

ACKNOWLEDGEMENTS

This book would not have been possible without the help of many people.

My interviewees, whose input was invaluable in shaping the book: Kathleen Campbell, Dr Maxine Daniels, Colette Engstrom, Carol Evans, Maryna Wolf Fontenoy, Janice Jacquet, Karen Liebenberg, Kim Marshall, Lisa Plutoni and Janine Kathleen Shapiro.

Ladies, you are the stars of this book. And why I know *Forward After Fifty* can be one of the most satisfying periods of one's life. Your strength and experience have inspired me; thank you for sharing your stories.

* * *

My reviewers, who painstakingly went through every word and gave me constructive feedback for improvement:

Carolyne Kauser Abbott, Claire McAlpine, Sabine Copinga, Alison Dunaway, Thea Hemery and Ana Onatah.

Your valuable time and thoughts have added the clarity and objectivity that is hard to see when you are so close to a piece of work that no one else has seen. Thank you for helping me improve this book from many angles and directions.

* * *

My team, Mark Beaumont-Thomas, my editor, whose attention to detail and constructive feedback has been indispensable.

Rhea Monte created the workbooks and graphics to make this final book beautiful to read.

Claire Macintyre professional photographer, whose time and talent produced all the photos.

Sam Pearce of SWATT Books for her guidance, incredible project management skills, and for helping me navigate self-publishing to get this book out into the world.

Ruby McGuire my writing coach and mentor whose suggestion to write a book sent me on a life-changing adventure. Her time, inspiration and belief in my mission made this book a reality.

Finally, I thank my partner in life, Alain Poirot, for cheering me on with positivity and humour.

Lightning Source UK Ltd.
Milton Keynes UK
UKHW020736301122
413110UK00011B/385

9 791041 505005